Silent Scream
Surviving a Mother's Nightmare Through Faith

A Memoir

Katherine Bailey

Dedication

For my daughter,

Elizabeth Katherine Stocker

Acknowledgment

I am grateful to the remarkable medical teams who played a crucial role in Liz's care. To the dedicated doctors and nurses at Mercy Health Emergency Room and Mercy Health Muskegon, your tireless efforts and expertise were invaluable. Special thanks to the compassionate staff at Select Care Specialty Hospital and Mary Free Bed Rehabilitation Hospital in Grand Rapids, Michigan, for their exceptional care and support.

I am profoundly grateful to my husband, Mark, whose unwavering support and faith were a source of strength during this challenging journey.

Finally, I want to express my deepest appreciation to our friends and family who offered support and prayers for Liz's recovery. Your love and prayers sustained us through the darkest days; we are eternally grateful for that.

About the Author

Katherine Korte Bailey Pursley, a resilient mother of four children and a stepdaughter, along with being a grandmother of fifteen, resides in Spring Lake, Michigan.

While this book marks her debut as an author, Katherine's journey through the harrowing experience of nearly losing a child has inspired her to share her story of faith, hope, and resilience.

Driven by her steadfast faith in the power of prayer and the divine, Katherine poured her heart and soul into this work, seeking solace and closure from the tribulation that tested her to the core.

Although she may never embark on another literary endeavor, Katherine's profound hope is that her story will offer consolation and inspiration to others, reminding them to trust in God's plan and the strength of the human spirit.

Preface

"Silent Scream: Living a Mother's Nightmare Through Faith" is a poignant exploration of a family's journey through a harrowing health crisis. This memoir delves deep into the emotional and physical turmoil experienced by those directly impacted by a life-altering medical event. From the initial shock of the emergency to the arduous path of recovery, the narrative offers a raw and honest portrayal of the challenges faced by the family.

Beyond the personal narrative, this book aims to shed light on the complexities of navigating the healthcare system, the importance of family support, and indomitable fortitude. It provides a glimpse into the emotional rollercoaster experienced by caregivers, the significance of hope and resilience, and the enduring power of human connection. It aims to convey that through shared experiences and collective strength, families can navigate even the most challenging of circumstances.

Ultimately, this memoir is a testament to the human capacity for love, perseverance, and healing. It is a story of survival, hope, and the unbreakable bonds of family. By sharing their journey, the author hopes to offer support and inspiration to others facing similar challenges, demonstrating that there is always a path forward, even in the darkest times.

It seeks to illuminate the complexities of a medical crisis, offering readers a profound understanding of the emotional and practical challenges families face during such times. It is a call to hope, resilience, and the enduring power of unwavering courage.

Contents

Dedication...i
Acknowledgment...ii
About the Author iii
Preface iv
Chapter 1: The Night Everything Changed 1
Chapter 2: Whispers Turn to Worries...................................... 11
Chapter 3: First Hours in the Hospital..................................... 27
Chapter 4: Waiting and Hoping... 40
Chapter 5: Setbacks and Strengths.. 53
Chapter 6: Glimmers of Recovery 71
Chapter 7: Long Road to Rehabilitation 82
Chapter 8: A New Beginning 107
Chapter 9: A Miracle from God... 125
Chapter 10: Reflections and Realizations............................... 136
Chapter 11: Messages of Gratitude and Hope 146
Chapter 12: Looking to the Future... 158
From the Care Pages... 168

Chapter 1: The Night Everything Changed

Life has a way of surprising us, sometimes in the gentlest ways, other times with a force that leaves us breathless. We often find ourselves lulled into a sense of security, pushing away the whispers of worry that persist in our minds.

We convince ourselves that our worst fears are shadows and figments of an overactive imagination. It's in these moments of perceived calm, when we least expect it, that the ground shifts beneath our feet.

A sudden storm rolls in, leaving devastation in its wake. In the aftermath, we are forced to confront the harsh reality that life doesn't always follow the script we write in our heads. It is in instances of unexpected hardship such as these that our strength is truly put to the test.

When I was only seventeen, my beloved father died of a massive heart attack while at work. He had been my rock, someone I loved dearly, and I was left with only his memories. From that day onwards, I began to think that these losses made me exempt from future tragedies and wrenching experiences.

However, little did I know then of the pain that would follow. A few years down the line, I lost my best friend to suicide, whom I had known since I was twelve. Later, another good friend of mine, who happened to be my children's teacher, died of lung cancer. I was in the room where she died, watching her slip away on the bed. The individual whose beautiful soul I had adored for so long was fading in front of me while I sat there, helpless before fate.

Although all the suffering had truly been theirs to endure, it deeply affected me. There was indeed some comfort in knowing that their pain must have finally subsided and that they were in a better place.

Perhaps I would continue to carry these tormenting memories of the past until the end of time. While it would have been natural to think God had tested me enough, the worst was yet to come.

Despite my share of mistakes in life, having children has never been a regret. Motherhood felt like my true calling, a constant source of love and purpose, with my children bringing immense joy along with their endless needs.

However, I never anticipated the flip side of that love: the potential for heart-wrenching pain. While the human capacity for resilience is remarkable, some fears tend to pierce through our defenses with a primal intensity. One among these is the thought of losing a child. It's an intangible suffering, an emotional undertow that pulls you under just as you resurface for air.

It is like a wave of heartache and distress that crashes over you repeatedly, leaving you gasping for breath while you drown in the depths of emotional agony. "Oh God, you did not tell me I could feel so much pain!" I lamented as I witnessed the unwinding of my life, a descent into a bottomless well of despair.

It was February 15th, 2020—a seemingly ordinary Saturday that would irrevocably alter the course of my life. Huatulco, Mexico, had beckoned us with its turquoise waters and stunning beaches. Mark, our Canadian friends Leah, Scott, and Marlene, and I had spent a delightful day basking in the sun on Tangolunda Beach.

In retrospect, I believe a twist of fate, perhaps a nudge from a higher power, intervened that day.

Meanwhile, dinner plans were made, then casually abandoned in favor of a cozy evening spent cooking and reminiscing at our condo, feeling weary from a day spent under the sun. Perhaps it was the beauty of the location, the joy of wonderful company, or a subconscious appreciation for life's simple pleasures. Whatever the reason, that day seemed to hold a deep sense of contentment and carefree bliss.

A quiet longing, perhaps a subconscious desire to savor the moment, drew me to our little balcony. A glass of wine warmed my hands, its gentle heat mirroring the peace that settled over me. Mark must have sensed my mood, for I distinctly remember him appearing with a perfectly golden grilled cheese sandwich, a simple gesture that spoke volumes of his love and care. Life couldn't have felt better in that moment.

As the sun dipped below the horizon, a quiet longing to be near Mark prompted me to return to our room. The space was empty, but the rhythmic whoosh of the shower offered a comforting sense of his presence. I turned on the series, "Outlander," to fill the sudden silence around me. Other than the program, the only sound was the distant hiss of the ocean breeze. Then, the phone rang, piercing the stillness with its insistent ring.

I glanced down at the screen, noticing it was Mary, my youngest daughter, who was pregnant and due in three weeks. With a surge of excitement, I answered the call, fully expecting news of the baby's arrival. Little did I know this call would forever alter the trajectory of our lives.

"Mom, I am calling with not such good news," said Mary.

"What?" I asked, my heart dropping the moment she uttered those words.

Mary broke the silence again before I could even process what I had heard.

"Mom, it's Liz. She went into cardiac arrest and suffered from six more arrests and, consequently, several strokes. We need you and Mark to come home."

It was as if a monstrous weight had come crashing down on me, ingraining itself onto my face. Words seemed redundant in the face of such a devastating revelation. My hands began to tremble uncontrollably, the phone feeling heavy and slick.

"I have to get out of here," I mumbled, the words barely audible.

Mary was still on the phone. "We're not able to see her yet. She is in the ER at Mercy Hospital in Muskegon. The plan is to move her to the ICU once she is stabilized."

With a trembling hand, I managed to end the call. Just then, Mark emerged, a towel wrapped around his waist, and his eyes immediately fell on my distraught form. He needed no explanation; the raw distress radiating from me spoke volumes.

While I was unaware of it at the time, the situation had taken a more serious turn. Emerging from the ER, the doctor delivered difficult news to Mary, Emily, and Liz's husband, Patrick: Liz's young heart, battered by the initial cardiac arrest and subsequent episodes, was struggling to maintain a steady rhythm, and they were struggling to stabilize her.

Faced with the chilling reality of their sister's vulnerable condition, Mary and Emily, in a moment of agonizing clarity, decided to call me.

As I sat miles away, unaware of the gravity of the situation, it seemed as if a physical force had settled upon me. It felt like a crushing pressure that had squeezed the air from my lungs. Terror, sharp and primal, clawed at my insides. Every nerve in my body thrummed with anxiety, a high-pitched buzz that drowned out all rational thought. The world around me blurred, my focus narrowing to the single, horrifying image of my precious Liz, my child, stricken down by such a devastating illness.

The phone felt like a dead weight in my hand, every fiber of my being yearning to be by my daughter's side. There was a stabbing pain in my chest, and all I could do was release this pain by crying. I felt helpless, sitting in a different country and enjoying my life while my daughter was in the hospital, trying to win the battle between life and death.

Then, a gentle hand pressed on my shoulder. Mark stood there, his calm demeanor an anchor in the storm of my emotions. He somehow understood the depths of my despair before I could even utter a word. Words of comfort flowed from him like a soothing balm on my raw emotions.

"What can I do?" he repeated, consoling me.

Without a moment's hesitation, he sprang into action. He contacted our Canadian friends, Leah, Scott, and Marlene, and conveyed the situation's urgency. Demonstrating the kindness characteristic of true friends, they offered immediate support. Arrangements were made: a ride to the airport in the morning, our rented condo secured, and the owners notified of our unexpected departure.

At that moment, overwhelmed by fear and grief, I realized how fortunate I was to have Mark by my side, his strength and composure a lifeline in the face of the chaos. I had always appreciated my husband's support and care, but I realized how much I needed him at that moment, and he was everything he should have been for me. Strong as a rock and immovable as a mountain, he shielded me from pain and made a safe cocoon to let my emotions out.

I could barely have gotten up and booked a flight home if he had not been there. The horrifying reality of the state of affairs hammered against my already fragile composure. My brain kept replaying the moment of Mary's call in a continuous loop. A torrent of questions, each more urgent than the last, flooded my thoughts.

Should I pack up and leave for the airport right away?

Were there even flights available at this late hour?

Left in disarray, the condo presented another logistical hurdle: who would handle notifying the owners and ensuring *proper care?*

Who would tell our friends? I had to call them.

Yet, a more crucial concern grew at the very core of my being: Liz. *What was her current state? Had she been moved out of the emergency room?*

Each passing minute felt like an eternity, and the urge to redial Mary's number was a constant battle that raged within me. The line between pertinent concerns and irrational anxieties blurred, confusing me.

Ultimately, it was Mark who convinced me to go to bed. I tried closing my eyes; however, sleep evaded me as a billion thoughts invaded my mind. I was vacationing here in Mexico while my daughter was literally in a life-or-death situation in another part of the world.

Yet, I soon realized that my presence wouldn't alleviate the immediate crisis. No, what was needed now was clear focus and decisive action. I had to get myself together. I had to take Ambien to sleep quickly; I don't recall how I woke up. Although I remember talking to my daughter, Emily, her words seemed muffled, like distant echoes in a thick fog. She kept asking me about the flight reservation, and my replies were sluggish and hesitant.

Finally, through the haze, I managed to force out, "I... I made the reservation, but..." I trailed off mid-sentence, the weight of my confusion a heavy cloak around me.

All I knew was that everything was taken care of by the time I showered and was ready. The condo was all cleaned up, our luggage packed, and our flight from Huatulco to Detroit was booked; even though our car was in Chicago, it didn't matter because our son would pick us up at the Detroit Metro Airport.

Our friends stayed until we were checked in, and Marlene, being fluent in Spanish, handled communicating with the Delta agent and checking us in at the counter. I could perceive everything from my friend's and my husband's kindness to the agent's concern. And even though I was back up to date with my surroundings, I still felt distant from reality. I wanted to utter something, but the relentless reminder of life and death loomed over my head.

So, as we said our goodbyes at the gate, I couldn't help but panic and cry over the countless unknown possibilities that awaited my family and me.

Each agonizing minute of the flight stretched into an eternity, making it the most emotionally draining day I had ever endured. I never knew I could feel that much pain. As I gazed out at the endless expanse of clouds, a maelstrom of emotions spun within me as the plane carried me closer to the unknown.

Will we make it there in time?

Will I ever see her walk through my front door and say, "Hi, Mummy?"

Will she die, and will Mary name her baby after her?

How was Patrick? How were Paige and Liam doing?

Please, God, give me the strength to be strong for Pat, Liam, and Paige. How traumatized they must have been.

Chris was waiting for us at the airport, and we headed toward Muskegon. My heart was about to bounce out of my chest as I saw Chris' pale face. The exchange of glances was enough to articulate the worries each of us had for Liz. We wasted no time and headed straight to the hospital to see her.

All the while, my mind spun with varying thoughts: Was this some punishment? God gave me such a lovely daughter, my beautiful Liz, but what had my child done to suffer from such misfortune? She never hurt anyone, so why was God hurting her?

But then, I shook these feelings away. God loves all, and I had to put my trust in Him. He does what is best, and I only had to push through to see the rainbow between the darkened clouds.

"When I am afraid,

I put my trust

In you."

-Psalm 56: 3

Chapter 2: Whispers Turn to Worries

The winter chill couldn't hold a candle to the frost that settled over Liz's loved ones on February 15th, 2020. It is a date etched into all our hearts. The impact wasn't singular but a ripple on a still pond. It was a tidal wave crashing over those closest to her.

Among those who felt the weight of the ordeal most acutely was Patrick, her husband. As much as it pained him, he knew this was a new reality, a world painted in shades of grief. Shouldering his immense sorrow, he recognized the long road of healing stretched before them all.

Later, Patrick recounted Liz having a seemingly normal, restful day at home. With their daughter Paige enjoying time with friends, he had taken their son Liam to a birthday party that afternoon.

Meanwhile, Mary had stopped by Liz's house around midday. She had brought some homemade spinach muffins, hoping they might help settle Liz's digestion. When Mary arrived, she found Liz relaxing in bed, watching a movie. Nothing appeared out of the ordinary.

As the evening unfolded, Patrick brought Liam home, who sprinted to join Liz in bed. It was around 6:45 PM when Liz texted Mary to thank her for the muffins, telling her they had indeed provided the relief she sought. Mary would later tell me that this was their last exchange for the day, and everything seemed calm and regular up to that point. Who could have known that a tragedy was about to strike merely hours later?

For a time, all seemed calm, but with a child's perceptive senses, young Liam began to feel something was amiss. When he turned to check on his mother, all his doubts were instantly confirmed. Shocked and horrified, Liam saw Liz's eyes starting to roll back. This wasn't any playful teasing or fun. What was overtaking Liz terrified her, evident in the distress in her eyes.

"Go, get Dad," she uttered weakly.

Liam sprinted out of the room to alert his dad as soon as his mother uttered those words. Patrick responded immediately and found Liz unresponsive, with her eyes rolled back. He yelled, proceeding to shake her. When Liz didn't respond, he immediately called 911 and was told to pull her to the floor and start CPR. Liam and Paige started crying, and Patrick told them to go to Paige's room and put Sullivan, the dog, in his cage.

It was about eight when the Sheriff's Department entered through the door. They pushed him out of the way and took over CPR. EMTs, the fire department, and the Sheriff were assisting however they could. They took Patrick to the kitchen for an "interview," where he was asked to explain about Liz's surgery the previous Monday. Duly, Patrick informed them that it had been a much-needed gynecological surgery involving a hysterectomy and bladder suspension.

Soon enough, Rachael, their neighbor, arrived to get the kids. Paige and Liam were horror-stricken by what had happened to their mother, and Rachael thought it was best to keep them safe -somewhere far from the scene to ease some of their worries. Later, Patrick called Mary and Emily and said Liz had an episode at home, and he was unsure what was happening.

As it happened, EMTs worked on Liz for about 45 minutes to stabilize her. Then, she was transported to Mercy Health Emergency Room in Muskegon, Michigan. Just when they thought things couldn't get any worse, Patrick was told that Liz had undergone another cardiac arrest on the way to the hospital.

Understandably, Patrick was lost, trying to figure out what to bring to the hospital before leaving. He tried to act strong, but his front was crumbling. Liz was everything to him, and if anything were to happen to her, he wouldn't be able to live with himself. The car ride to the hospital was a difficult one, brewing thoughts that haunted him, but he had to keep faith.

Plagued by similar anxieties, Mary clung to the memory of Liz's text about the muffins, a mundane detail that now loomed large as their last conversation that day.

The evening had begun normally for her, brimming with bedtime routines. While Mary's husband, Paul, tucked the boys into bed upstairs, Mary curled up on the couch downstairs, having a quiet moment. Then, a notification chimed on her phone, shattering the tranquility of the atmosphere. It was a text from Emily.

"Hey! You heading over to the Stockers' tonight?" the message read.

"No, why? Everything okay?" Mary typed out a quick reply.

There was a beat of silence, followed by a flurry of texts from Emily. Mary's heart lurched as she read them, each message masked with a growing sense of panic.

"Liz passed out!" one read. *"Pat just texted me."*

"He tried calling you and me, but neither of us picked up!" another followed.

Like a cold serpent, fright coiled around Mary, tightening with each beat of her heart. She scrambled to check her missed calls. And sure enough, there was a missed call from Patrick. Dread nibbled at her as she realized they had both missed his calls.

When she finally reached Patrick, his voice appeared choked with fear, confirming the arrival of the ambulance. The image of him flustered and grasping at straws for explanation mirrored the turmoil within herself. It was the abrupt end of that call that propelled Mary into action.

Panic surged through her like a jolt of electricity that drove her off the couch. Her house, a haven of peace merely moments ago, now felt like a cage closing in on her. A horrifying realization came crashing into her in a whirlwind of ten seconds: she had to get to Liz.

Upon reaching there, she saw the house eerily transformed. The sight that greeted her felt as if it had been ripped out of a nightmare. The familiar driveway was bathed in the harsh glare of flashing lights, red and blue strobing against a backdrop of worried faces. An ambulance sat squat in the center. Even from a distance, Mary could see several police cars parked haphazardly on the street, adding to the air of chaos.

As Mary walked inside, she instantly spotted Patrick. He appeared like a statue sculpted from grief, unable to offer anything but a bewildered shake of his head. Meanwhile, paramedics emerged, carrying Liz in a sling, choking Mary with fear. Her sister, usually vibrant and full of life, lay unnervingly still.

In those circumstances, the paramedics' words offered at least a flicker of hope: stable blood pressure, breathing on her own. But the unanswered question hung heavy in the air: *was Liz even conscious?*

She desperately craved answers to pierce the suffocating terror.

Just then, the weight of responsibility settled heavily on her shoulders. With a heart heavy with worry, she crossed the street to Rachael's to check on the children. She knew the children would be confused, their young minds already struggling with the unsettling turn of events.

Throughout this time, Patrick wrestled with his anxieties. Lost in a daze, he rummaged through drawers, occupied with the mundane task of packing a hospital bag. When Mary entered the room and sensed his disheveled state, her gaze instantly filled with concern.

"Do you want me to drive you?" she asked gently.

Patrick shook his head. "No, I'll be alright," he mumbled, his words lacking conviction.

A silent understanding seemed to pass between them. They both knew "alright" was a distant possibility at that moment. So, a hurried plan was hatched. Mary would settle the children for the night, then head to the hospital herself. Alone with her thoughts, she steeled herself for the coming battle to hold onto hope in the face of the unknown.

Then came a knock on the door, cutting through the tense silence. As if fate itself offered continual support, and right when Mary needed it most, Colin, Emily's husband, along with his daughters, Bailey and Lyla, showed up at the door. In a flurry of hushed voices, Mary filled them in on the limited details she knew.

Bailey offered to stay at Liz and Pat's house for the night without even being asked. This meant the kids wouldn't have to be moved and could sleep in their own beds, feeling safe and sound during this challenging time.

With a grateful nod to Bailey, Mary finally allowed herself a moment to breathe. The night felt heavy, like a thick blanket pressing down on them.

Emily was working the night shift at the hospital when she missed Patrick's text and call. The final message read, "EMS is here."

Emily's heart raced with worry. She quickly reached out to her husband, Colin, urging him to rush to Liz's house. As Colin and her daughter, Bailey, hurried to the scene, Emily's mind whined with concern for Liz and her family.

By the time Colin and Bailey arrived at Liz and Pat's home, Liz was already being carried out in a sling by the paramedics. Emily's anxiety peaked as she spoke with Mary over the phone, learning that Mary and Patrick were bound for the hospital together.

An hour had crawled by for Mary since she arrived at Mercy ER in Muskegon.

She called Emily again, urging her to leave work as they still hadn't seen Liz. Emily quickly arranged for coverage at the hospital and then left Grand Rapids for Muskegon. The journey was fraught with nervousness, the icy roads mirroring the chill in Emily's heart. Nowhere was the feeling more potent than in the car hurtling down towards the hospital.

On that Saturday night, when the chilling news reached him through Emily's text, Chris, Liz's brother, felt the weight of the world crashing down upon him. The blood drained from his face, and the text from Emily informing him of Liz's situation shattered the normalcy of his evening.

As he scrambled to get more information, a horrifying image flashed into his mind: his niece and nephew, traumatized, fearing for their mother's life. The gravity of the situation and the helplessness of being so far away bore down on him. He had to get to them, to be there for his family in their time of need.

Realistically assessing the situation, Chris realized he couldn't drive himself. The responsibility made the choice clear. He decided to rely on his wife, Alexis, and whisk their children away to her sister before heading their way toward the hospital.

Later, when Alexis recounted the events of that harrowing night, she couldn't help but reflect on her own experiences. On February 15th, 2020, she was nestled in bed, seeking comfort in the familiar glow of her Netflix screen. Meanwhile, Chris occupied himself in the cigar room. With the children already fast asleep, the house was filled with calmness.

However, the tranquility was shattered when Chris suddenly appeared, his demeanor laced with a sense of urgency. Confused by his inquiries about Liz's recent hysterectomy, which they had discussed earlier that day, Alexis brushed it off as the effects of Chris' indulgence in a few gin and tonics. However, unease seemed to creep in on her, hinting at the awaiting storm about to descend upon their lives. *What had happened to Liz?* It was all she could manage to think.

Confusion and concern clouded Alexis' thoughts as she questioned Chris about his sudden interest in Liz's recent surgery. Then, Chris revealed the alarming text message he had received, informing him that Liz had passed out at home. However, Alexis' phone, set to "do not disturb" after 9:00 PM, had kept her oblivious to the news.

Initially, they underestimated the gravity of the situation, attributing Liz's fainting spell to post-surgery weakness. The true extent of the severity of her condition hadn't fully sunk in yet, and they reassured themselves, thinking it was merely a minor setback in Liz's recovery journey.

However, despite their attempts to rationalize the situation, a seed of concern began to sprout, hinting at the uncertainty descending upon their lives. Alexis knew their peaceful evening had come to an abrupt end, her mind racing with anxiety.

Soon enough, the unsettling silence between her and Chris was disrupted by Emily's phone call to him, delivering the jarring news that Liz hadn't just passed out but had suffered a cardiac arrest.

Cardiac arrest.

The words struck them like a thunderbolt, prompting urgent discussions about whether to rush to the hospital.

Feeling desperate, they decided to wait for more information before deciding. However, as time ticked by, their concern only intensified. When Mary's call finally came, revealing the seriousness of Liz's condition, they knew they had no choice but to act.

After arranging for their children's care and saying a silent prayer for Liz's well-being, they began the journey to the hospital. The drive passed in silence, broken only by the sound of their racing thoughts and keen hopes for a positive outcome. All they could do was hold on to a frantic desire to find Liz, not in a sterile hospital bed hooked to machines, but sitting up, laughing; the terrifying torment a distant memory.

Looking back on it now, the night's chaos reverberated through the entire family. For Bailey, though, February 15th started much differently. It was a Saturday, and a new blossoming relationship in her life cast a rosy glow on the day after Valentine's, with fresh flowers sitting proudly in her room.

But amidst the happiness, a nagging feeling, an inexplicable urge, troubled her. She hadn't yet confided in Aunt Liz about her new love, and the silence felt heavy. She knew texting wouldn't suffice and needed to see her aunt to discuss this new chapter in person.

With a determined glint in her eye, Bailey texted Liz, checking in after her surgery and asking if a visit would be all right. The reply came swiftly: a simple "yes" and a reassuring note about the unlocked front door. Little did Bailey know that short exchange would be stamped in her memory forever, the last written communication with her beloved aunt before the world tilted on its axis.

Her heart ached as she recalled the familiar scene of arriving at Liz's home and finding her in bed, watching a movie. With the rest of the family temporarily absent, they cherished those precious moments together, just like old times. Liz's comforting presence had always been a source of relief for Bailey, a reassuring constant in her life.

As they conversed, Bailey found the usual comfort in Aunt Liz's understanding and support, grateful for the opportunity to confide in someone who truly listened.

Then, she could not have known how the idyllic afternoon would be shattered later that evening. Dinner with her dad and sister was a blur, the carefree chatter replaced by unease. The phone call that interrupted their drive home was a punch in the gut. Her mom, Emily, a nurse practitioner, sounded uncharacteristically stressed on the other end.

When her dad hung up, a single phrase hung heavy: "Something with Aunt Liz."

Confusion tore at Bailey as her father dialed another number, his brow furrowed in concern. His brief conversation with Mary only deepened the mystery. Her aunt's voice, usually cheerful and strong, was strained and frantic. The abrupt end of the call sent a shiver down Bailey's spine before her dad could even finish his sentence.

At once, instinct took over. They veered off course to the familiar path leading to the Stockers' house. The closer they got, the more the pieces clicked into place, forming a picture far more terrifying than she could have imagined. Pulling into the driveway, the sight of the departing ambulance confirmed her worst fears.

This wasn't a minor setback. This was serious.

When they emerged from the car, Patrick was already heading out. Her dad's attempts to talk to him seemed to fall on deaf ears. But could you blame him?

The flashing lights of the ambulance and the discomforting chaos settled heavily on Bailey's heart and threatened to consume her. The carefree girl who had rejoiced in her aunt's company just hours earlier was gone, replaced by a young woman facing a reality she was nowhere near prepared for.

They returned home in what was a brief interlude in the unfolding drama. Back at the Stockers' house, Bailey found herself alone, willingly taking responsibility for shielding her younger cousins, Paige and Liam, from the disorder brewing around them.

Flicking on the TV, Bailey put on a movie, a desperate attempt to regain normalcy. But the animated characters on the screen seemed to mock the grim reality. Paige, usually chatty and energetic, was withdrawn, while Liam, sensing the underlying tension, verbalized the unspoken fear that pecked at them all.

"So, is my mom going to die?"

His innocent question, masked with a child's vulnerability, crushed the fragile facade Bailey had built. Tears welled up in her eyes, blurring her vision.

"I don't know," she choked out, the words a bitter truth. The knowledge of their ignorance, their lack of answers, was a cruel twist of the knife.

Suddenly, Liam's next words pierced the veil of confusion. He spoke of watching a movie with his mom, the memory fresh in his young mind. His description of her, "looked like she had died," sent a fresh wave of terror crashing over Bailey. The image of his dad, frantic and desperate, shaking his mom awake while dialing for help, painted another horrific picture in his mind. At this point, the weight of the revelation was almost unbearable.

Instructed to shield her younger cousins from the harsh reality, Bailey found herself playing a role she wasn't prepared for. Steeling herself, she retreated downstairs, the forced smile replaced by a grimace of despair. The phone felt heavy in her hand as she dialed her dad's number.

"Dad?" Her voice trembled.

Silence stretched on the other end, feeling like an eternity. Then, her dad's voice filled the void.

"Hey, Bailey. Are you okay?"

Then, the dam broke. Tears streamed down her face, momentarily blinding her. The weight of the secret, the fear for her aunt, the overwhelming helplessness; it all came crashing down in a torrent of choked sobs.

"Can I stay the night?" she stammered between breaths.

"Of course, honey," her dad replied. "If that's what you want. We're all in this together."

With his consent, Bailey felt relief wash over her, and she was grateful for the opportunity to be there for her family in their time of need.

Steadily, the house settled into an uneasy quiet as Paige and Liam drifted off to sleep, reassured by Bailey's reassurances. Yet, the weight of her lie bore heavily on her. Even Sully, the usually boisterous family dog, seemed to sense the turmoil. His playful energy seemed dimmed, replaced by a restless pacing. His worried brown eyes, searching for Liz, mirrored the anxiety that choked the house.

Sleep evaded Bailey for most of the night. The silence throbbed in her ears, punctuated only by the soft tick of the clock and Sully's quiet footsteps following her every move. Exhaustion gnawed at her, but the fear for her aunt was a potent stimulant.

Then, the phone rang, and Alexis' voice crackled through the receiver.

"Bailey, honey," Alexis said, "we're on our way from Detroit. Listen, don't try to be an adult here. You're scared, and that's okay. If you need anything at all, promise me you'll call. Don't be afraid to ask for help."

Just then, the show of forced strength crumbled, replaced by a vulnerability she hadn't dared to acknowledge. Bailey knew that she wasn't the protector, not tonight. She was a scared child, lost in a storm, and it was okay to ask for help.

Lyla's account of events mirrored Bailey's in many ways. She recalled shopping with her sister and father, enjoying a meal together before their world was suddenly rocked by a phone call from their mother, Emily.

Like Bailey, Lyla initially dismissed the severity of the situation. Perhaps Liz's heart had fluttered for a moment, a minor scare. Relief washed over them, albeit temporarily. They decided to check in on their aunt just to be safe.

However, a sense of dread coiled in Lyla's stomach once they pulled into the familiar driveway. The sight of a departing ambulance confirmed her worst fears - this wasn't a minor blip.

Tears welled up in her eyes, mirroring Bailey's silent sobs. The carefree afternoon and the shared laughter all seemed a lifetime ago. At that moment, the weight of the situation crashed down on her, plunging them into a state of shock and disbelief.

With heavy hearts, Lyla and her father made the difficult decision to return home, leaving Bailey to stay the night at Liz's house, providing comfort and support to the children while their mother was taken by ambulance to the hospital.

The news of Liz's sudden illness spread like wildfire, swiftly coursing through the family and reaching even Elizabeth, Liz's stepsister. The first tremor came in the form of a text from Emily, likely relaying the initial details of the scare as she understood them. This was then followed by a frantic phone call from Mark, Elizabeth's father, as he filled her in on the unfolding situation.

The impending trip to Breckenridge added another layer of guilt to her already heavy heart, knowing that she couldn't be there for Liz, and with each passing moment, the distance felt like an insurmountable chasm.

That Sunday stretched into infinity, interrupted by tearful phone calls, panicked whispers, and a fear that twisted tightly in Elizabeth's gut. The joy of the planned vacation had evaporated, replaced by a suffocating atmosphere of worry and the crushing weight of the unknown. All she could do was wait, holding on to the flimsy hope that somehow, someway, things would be alright.

Wouldn't that be what each of us wanted? she thought. To wake up from this horrifying nightmare and see Liz back in her usual radiant self. The desire for a simple return to the life we once knew, a life filled with love, laughter, and the comforting presence of our beloved Liz, became a silent prayer that resonated deep within each of our hearts.

Chapter 3: First Hours in the Hospital

The first few days following that harrowing night stretched out like an eternity, shrouded in fear and despair. They were days we would forever wish to erase from memory, brimming with a pain that seemed almost impossible to bear. Witnessing our beloved Liz wrestle with her health was agonizing for us, and each labored breath she took was a fresh stab in our hearts.

The vibrant laughter that once filled our lives had been instantly replaced by a chilling silence, broken only by the sterile hum of hospital equipment and the choked sobs of loved ones. It was a time when the very foundation of our world seemed to crumble, leaving us floating in a sea of uncertainty, clinging to the feeble hopes for a miracle.

Then came the distressing wait during the first hours in the hospital. Having hurried through the hospital halls, Mary finally found herself in a small waiting room. Patrick was already there, with lines of worry engraved on his face. A kind chaplain greeted them, offering words of comfort that sounded like a lifeline amid their raging storm of emotions.

However, the subsequent arrival of the ER doctor brought a new wave of anxiety. His verdict confirmed their worst fears: Liz had suffered additional episodes on the way to the hospital, and they were working desperately to stabilize her.

His departure left a heavy silence, with Mary and Patrick devastated even though they had been told so beforehand.

Just what had triggered these multiple cardiac arrests? The question nibbled at them like a persistent repeat in silence. It was a dilemma that embedded itself in my own heart when I learned of Liz's condition.

Yet, the very first revelations of Liz's condition in that sterile waiting room gave rise to a battle, one between crippling despair and a desperate hope that somehow, someway, things would turn in her favor.

Following the first encounter with the doctor, a suffocating silence pressed down on them as they sat huddled together. Then, Patrick's voice suddenly broke the oppressive quiet, and he began recounting the initial events at home.

"I found her in the bedroom," he began. "She was... convulsing, Mary. Making these awful gurgling sounds, her teeth clenched tight, and..." His voice cracked slightly. "Her eyes... they were rolling back in her head."

Mary listened, her heart clenching with each word. She couldn't imagine the terror Liz must have experienced in those traumatic moments. A wave of nausea washed over her, and the walls of the waiting room seemed to close in on her with an overpowering fear. Clutching the phone tighter, she walked down the hall to update Alexis and Chris about Liz's condition.

"The doctor..." Mary began. "He said they're struggling to keep Liz's heart stable. They need more tests, but..."

Her voice trailed off before she finally managed to speak again.

"Lex, it's bad," a choked sob escaped her lips.

Suddenly, she spotted the ER doctor heading toward the waiting room with concern on his face.

"Gotta go," Mary whispered, hanging up the phone.

Heavily pregnant, her legs felt laden with a different kind of weight as she hurried toward the waiting room. The doctor's words boomed in her mind as he explained their difficulties.

"We're having a hard time keeping her heart rate stable," he said. "There are a few things it could be, but we need to run more tests to get a clearer picture."

"What... what does this mean?" Mary stammered.

The doctor sighed, his eyes filled with empathy.

"Right now, it's too early to say. We need to focus on stabilizing her first. Then, we can investigate the cause more deeply."

Upon his departure, the room plunged into a profound silence. A single, shared glance between Mary and Patrick spoke volumes. Tears welled in their eyes, spilling over soundlessly, for it was a moment that surpassed the need for words. The sliver of hope they had desperately held on to seemed to die, replaced by a chilling fear that seeped deep into their bones. The battle within them shifted dramatically, threatening to smother the remaining flimsy ash of optimism.

Hours bled into one another, interrupted only by the rhythmic beeping of unseen machines. Weary and lost, Mary and Patrick clung to each other until a familiar face appeared. It was Emily, with dread evident on her face as she entered the room.

Meanwhile, the doctor's words echoed in Mary and Patrick's minds like an endless loop of grim possibilities. Seeing Liz and spotting any sign of normalcy was all they craved. Since the ambulance had rushed her away, they had been left with nothing but a cavernous void and hollow promises.

While the hospital chaplain's kind words offered a temporary balm on their raw wounds, the medical updates continued to be vague, only deepening their anxiety.

Finally, at eleven o'clock that night, Dr. Eric Sandy emerged from Liz's room. Recognition sparkled briefly in Emily's eyes; she knew him from her clinical rotations at Metro Hospital.

Dr. Sandy took a deep breath before speaking.

"Look," he said, "we've been doing everything we can, but Liz's condition is critical. There are some tough decisions you may need to make..."

His words sounded like a death knell to the fragile ray of optimism they had desperately held onto. Tears flowed anew as a fresh wave of grief overpowered them. The tide had turned, and apparently not in their favor. But just as misery threatened to overcome them, a hint of relief emerged: they would finally see Liz.

Thirty unbearable minutes later, the trauma bay doors finally slid open. The harsh fluorescent lights blinded their eyes as they entered the vast, sterile space. Dr. Sandy stood beside Liz, along with two male nurses and a male respiratory therapist, who bustled around her.

And then their eyes fell on Liz. *Liz.* There she was, pale and fragile, a tangle of tubes and wires snaking across her body. She was barely recognizable; however, she appeared amazingly beautiful. Just as the trio circled her, they noticed a trace of movement; her right arm twitched slightly in a defiant struggle against the restricting tube. The nurses reacted immediately, administering more sedation with evident urgency.

"It took us a while to stabilize her," a nurse explained. "That's why you couldn't see her sooner. Every time we tried to take her for a CT scan, her heart would go into arrhythmia."

Their next step was getting Liz to the ICU, but her condition remained too unstable for transport. Disappointment consumed them, a bitter aftertaste to the tentative hope they had dared to embrace.

"We'll let you know as soon as she's stable enough to be moved," Dr. Sandy said gently. "For now, you'll need to wait outside."

With heavy hearts, Mary, Emily, and Patrick shuffled out of the trauma bay. The hospital walls seemed to mock their despair, offering no consolation for the chaos churning within them. They huddled together, seeking support in each other's presence as their eyes filled with a silent plea for a miracle.

It was not until around midnight that an outbreak of activity broke the consuming silence. *Liz was being transferred to the ICU.*

Meanwhile, news of Liz's condition had reached everyone, including her father, Gary, who was on his way to the hospital. Knowing his support was crucial, Emily excused herself to the general waiting area. Left alone, Mary and Patrick followed Emily to the waiting area, knowing Liz was being transferred and they would have to wait a while before seeing her again.

The stressful wait stretched on, and finally, they were permitted to see Liz at one o'clock in the morning. The ICU doors swung open, revealing a starkly lit room filled with medical equipment. Liz lay there, a fragile figure nestled among the whirring machines and blinking lights. They watched, hearts heavy with relief and dread, as the nurses fussed over her, getting her settled in.

The sight of their beloved Liz, pale and vulnerable, sent a tremor of raw fear through them. But even in the face of overwhelming distress, they knew they would not give up on Liz. They would fight alongside her every step of the way. The steadfast resolve in their hearts was their only weapon against the tide of terror gnawing at their insides.

At approximately two in the morning, Chris and Alexis arrived at the hospital, weary but determined. A kind nurse led them to the ICU waiting room, where Mary and Emily sat. Patrick, they were told, was by Liz's side.

A tearful reunion ensued as Mary and Emily filled Chris and Alexis in on the painful hours they had endured. Then, with a deep sigh, they led them to Liz's room. Stepping through the doorway, the unadulterated reality of the situation hit Chris and Alexis with a gut-wrenching force.

The room was dimly lit in stark contrast with the brightness of the waiting area. But even in the subdued light, Liz's condition was painfully clear. The very sight of her stole the air from their lungs, settling on their chests like a crushing weight.

She lay motionless, nuzzled in a tangle of tubes and wires twisting across her fragile form. Her pale skin and shallow breaths depicted a woman far removed from the vibrant Liz they all knew. It was a nightmarish scene that would forever be ingrained in their memories.

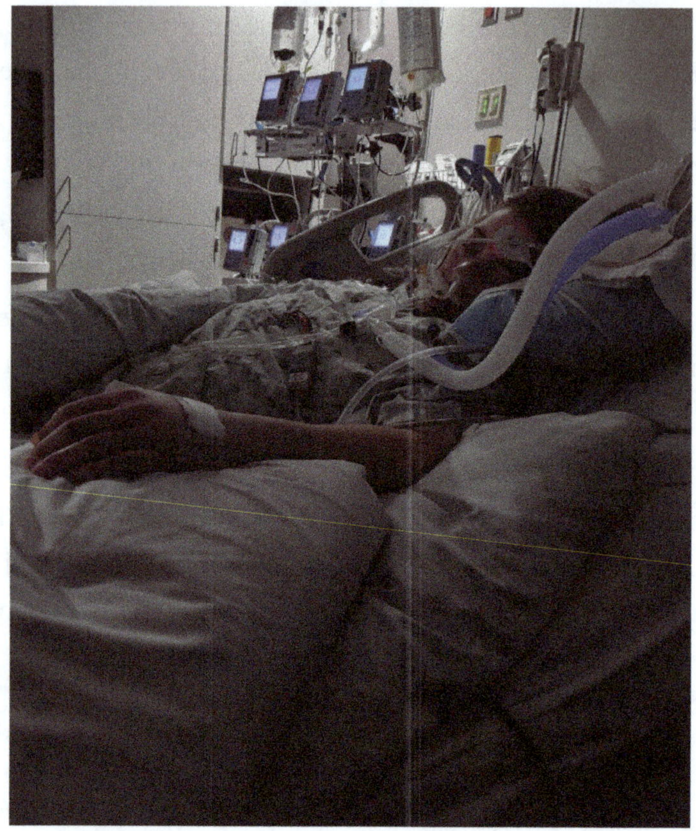

After a while, the others filed out, and the room abounded with the familiar sore silence. The weariness of this night, which now seemed perennial, pressed in on them. Just then, Alexis saw the exhaustion engraved on Patrick's face.

"You should get some rest, Patrick," she said gently.

He shook his head stubbornly. "No, I can't leave her side."

"We'll be here for her together," Alexis reassured him. "But you need to take care of yourself too."

Patrick hesitated, his gaze lingering on Liz's pale face.

"I don't want to leave her alone," he said.

A flicker of understanding dawned on Alexis.

"I know," she murmured, placing a comforting hand on his arm. "I wouldn't dream of leaving you either. We'll stay here, both of us."

A trace of relief flashed in Patrick's eyes, finding comfort in her presence. Side by side, they sat in the quiet room. As it happened, their quiet vigil was shattered moments later by a burst of movement. Alarms blared, and nurses rushed in with grim expressions, driving them out into the hallway.

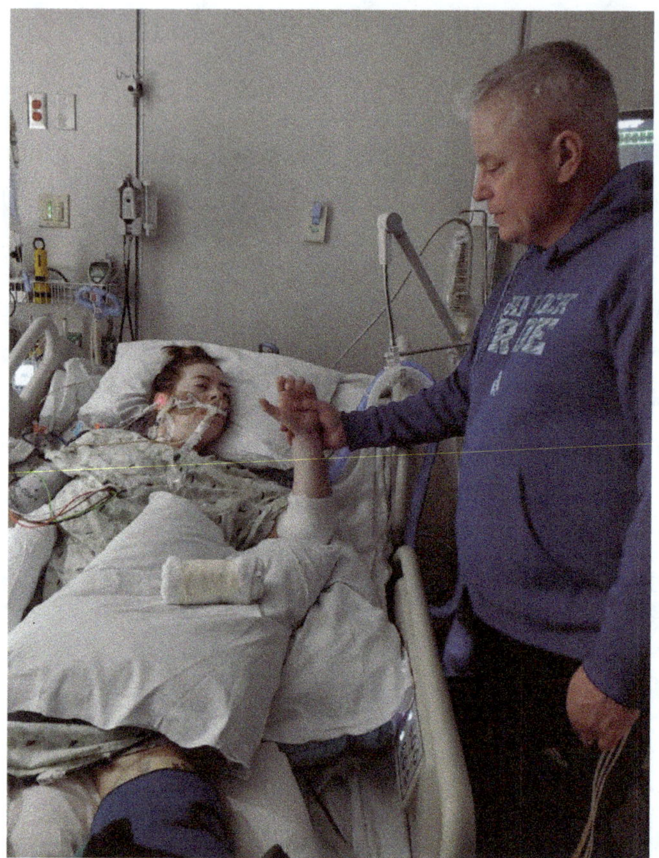

Something was wrong with Liz. Panic surged through Patrick and Alexis, gripping their hearts. Patrick's hand tightened around Alexis'.

"What's happening?" he rasped.

Alexis swallowed the lump in her throat, forcing a reassuring smile. "Liz is strong, Patrick. She's getting the best care possible. They'll take care of her."

Her words were meant to comfort him, but they rang hollow even to her ears. The ICU room felt like a prison, and as Alexis watched Liz, a wave of helplessness washed over her. But then, she saw Patrick. His face, usually so full of life, was marked with evident worry, and his shoulders slumped in defeat. Suddenly, a fierce sense of protectiveness flared within her: she wouldn't let fear paralyze them. She had to be strong for Liz and Patrick.

But Patrick's legs gave way before she could act upon her resolve. With a choked gasp, he slid down the wall, his face crumpled with fatigue and fear. Alexis reacted instinctively, catching him before he hit the floor. Together, they sank to a crouch, backs pressed against the cold wall.

Just then, a kind nurse appeared, a concerned frown creasing her forehead. "Here, sir," she said gently, placing a chair beside Patrick. "Have a seat. Can I get you some water?"

Patrick nodded numbly, accepting the water with a trembling hand. Alexis sat beside him and wrapped her arm around his shoulder. They were in the eye of the storm, beaten and bruised, but they wouldn't break. For Liz, they would weather it no matter how impossible it seemed.

Exhaustion grew on them, reminding them of the road of suffering ahead. But the thought of leaving Liz's side was unthinkable. As the night progressed, Chris and Mary decided to head home for a few hours of rest while Emily and Alexis stayed with Patrick. With Liz at the center of their world, Emily and Alexis vowed to hold the fort and stay strong.

The night wore on, a long, slow crawl marked by stolen moments of sleep and the constant hum of the machines.

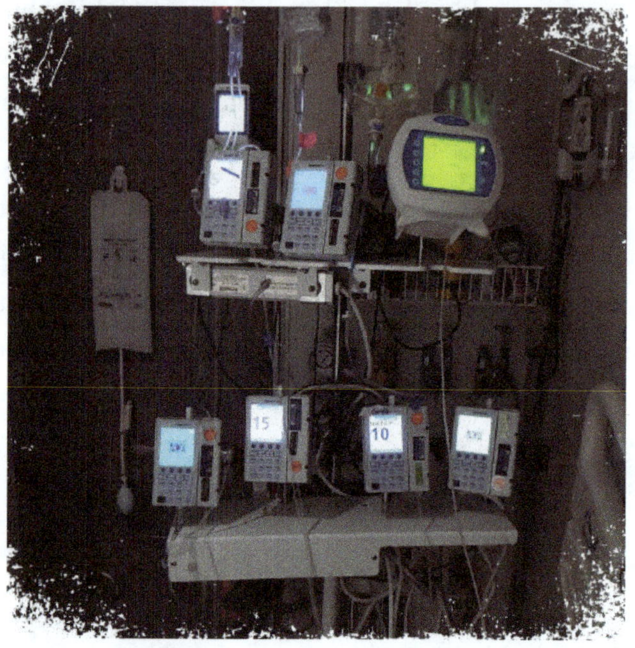

Then, a soft rustle moved them from their uneasy slumber. A nurse entered the room with quick, practiced movements as she checked on Liz.

"I'm so sorry," the nurse murmured.

Alexis bristled. *Sorry?* What did she mean, *sorry?* Seeing the "sorry" expression on the nurse's face made Alexis' blood boil. Was this nurse giving up? Was she implying...?

The words choked in her throat like unspoken accusations. Yet, she forced herself to remain silent, biting back the fierce retort that signaled to escape.

The rest of the night passed in a blur. However, Alexis, Emily, and Patrick were determined not to let despair take root and to find the courage to face whatever came next.

Chapter 4: Waiting and Hoping

The following day felt like a completely different world from the one that had existed before. My journey back from Mexico to Detroit was a blur of disquiet, my mind a tangled mess of thoughts about my precious Liz and, of course, my grandchildren, Paige and Liam.

The previous night had been a nightmare for everyone, especially Bailey, who had to hold things together for the kids. As the morning dawned, a sliver of light peeked through the curtains, illuminating the room with a soft glow. Bailey stirred awake, with the revelations of the night pressing down on her chest.

Soon after, Colin arrived, a kind soul bearing the familiar comfort of McDonald's breakfast. However, the scene that greeted him was a sharp departure from the usual. Paige and Liam, usually enthusiastic eaters, barely glanced at their food. They sat there, quiet and withdrawn, like little ships lost at sea. Seeing the children so reserved, with their customary joy replaced by a chilling silence, was a punch in the gut that finally drove home the true impact of the situation.

The tumult that had swept through their lives had left a trail of devastation in its wake, and the road to recovery stretched long and uncertain before them.

Shortly after, Colin decided to take the children to his home, offering them a change of scenery and acknowledging they might need to stay there for a while.

Drained from the night's emotional toll, Bailey retreated to the shower, with the hot water washing away the grime but not the worry stamped on her face.

Downstairs, Lyla and Gabe found the children reserved. While they all indulged in video games, the joy seemed muted, almost gone. Paige sat quietly, not asking any questions. However, Liam, young and struggling to process the events, finally broke the silence.

"Is Mommy going to die?" he asked in a small, choked voice. "Will I have to go to a funeral?"

Lyla and Gabe exchanged a worried look, their hearts aching for the scared children. They knew the kids were traumatized. However, they were also aware that there weren't any easy answers to give at the moment, only the promise to be there for them every step of the way.

"The doctors are taking good care of your mom, buddy," Lyla said gently, kneeling to meet Liam's gaze. "We're all here for you."

The morning, once painted with hope, had become darker for everyone. Meanwhile, after carefully updating me on the situation at the hospital and acknowledging the update on our journey and our arrival time, Emily made her way to the ICU. Her stomach twisted with every step she took.

Upon reaching Liz's room with Rebecca, a fellow nurse, practitioner, and friend, a brand-new wave of dismay washed over her. News filtered through: Liz's condition had taken a turn for the worse. Outside Liz's door, a crash cart stood ready. It was a scary reminder of the grave situation.

Inside, Emily found Dr. Sandy and a PA huddled around Liz's bedside. The sight of her sister, pasty-faced and fragile, sent a fresh jolt of fear through Emily, indicating that whatever news these medical professionals held was not hopeful.

Despite the whirring machines she was supported by and the sedation being turned off, Liz seemed lost in a silent struggle. Her fight for life seemed to be hanging in the balance. She looked vastly different from the lively woman Emily knew.

"How is she, Dr. Sandy?" Emily asked.

Creases appeared on Dr. Sandy's face, exposing his concern.

"Her potassium level is dangerously high, Emily," he explained. "It's a common reaction to the stress her body is under, but it's worrisome."

The world started to spin for Emily.

"We're working to bring it down – a high level can lead to heart rhythm problems and even another cardiac arrest. It's a very critical time right now," Dr. Sandy continued.

Emily felt a cold dread seep into her bones. Her hands grew clammy, with a sickening sensation that reflected the fear nibbling at her insides.

Mom hasn't even seen her yet. This... this can't keep getting worse, can it?

As she stepped out of the ICU, an anxious plea reverberated in her mind, a quiet prayer for a miracle amidst the disorder she was plunging into. She needed to find Alexis to share the burden of this distressing state of affairs that threatened to immerse them all.

Meanwhile, Chris returned to the hospital, oblivious to the darkness that awaited him. One look at Emily's face shattered his hopeful façade. The air snapped with a tension that spoke of shattered hopes.

"What happened?" Chris asked. "Any news about Liz?"

Emily took a shaky breath.

"It's not good," she managed to say, the words scraping raw against her throat. "They reduced the sedation, hoping she'd wake up, but..."

Her voice trailed off, too afraid to speak the implicit.

"But?" Chris' curiosity grew.

"Liz is not breathing on her own. She's still intubated. Right now, all they can do is keep her stable."

The gravity of those words enveloped them both, a crushing reminder of the risky tightrope Liz was walking. Yet, they could only sit and wait, praying for a miracle.

Exhaustion, like a relentless tide, finally pulled at Emily. She needed to rest and steel herself for the long vigil ahead. With a heavy heart, she decided to head home for a few hours of sleep, vowing to return and be by Liz's side through the night.

As the day progressed, news sifted through Chris: Dr. Harris, the cardiologist, and Dr. Hager, the pulmonologist, were working tirelessly to keep Liz stable. Their goal was to gradually reduce the sedation, allowing them to assess her condition more accurately.

By midday, Emily returned to the hospital. There, she found Mary, who updated her on Liz's situation.

"Liz has taken a turn, rather more a frightening one – ventricular fibrillation. But thankfully, the medical team had managed to stabilize her without needing a defibrillator," Mary explained.

A hint of relief passed through Emily, quickly replaced by a new worry.

"The doctors need her to be more stable before they can continue lowering the sedation," Mary added. "Their goal is to wake her up in the next day or two, but they need to be cautious."

Cautious.

The word rang in their minds. Waking her up safely meant her body had to be strong enough to handle it. Every decision felt like taking a small step forward, blindfolded, with the risk of falling back at any moment.

Then came an echocardiogram, a painless procedure using sound waves to create an image of the heart. It provided a glimpse into Liz's struggling heart and revealed a troubling truth: its function had dipped to a critical 15-20%. This meant her heart muscle, responsible for pumping blood throughout her body, was struggling to do its job.

Dr. Harris suspected cardiomyopathy, a general term for a disease affecting the heart muscle. Cardiomyopathy can weaken the heart, making it difficult to pump blood efficiently. This can lead to fluid buildup in the lungs, fatigue, and shortness of breath, symptoms that mirrored Liz's current condition. However, the cause of Liz's cardiomyopathy remained unclear.

Just six days before this life event, Liz had undergone major gynecological surgery involving a hysterectomy and bladder suspension. A hysterectomy involves removing the uterus. Bladder suspension, on the other hand, is a procedure to correct a weakened pelvic floor, which can sometimes lead to problems with bladder control. While both procedures are relatively common, any surgery carries some risk, and doctors were now scrambling to understand if there might be a connection to Liz's current heart trouble.

As for the family, the path ahead seemed to twist and turn with each new development, leaving them with more questions than answers. Hope flickered like a candle in the wind, and for the most part, fear pecked at their hearts.

The doctors worked tirelessly, piecing together the puzzle of Liz's condition. Their expertise and dedication were evident in their approach to her care. Even her surgeon, who had performed her gynecological surgery on her, made a point to visit during her recovery. His concern and support were a testament to the collaborative nature of healthcare.

Slowly, updates began to trickle in, offering a trace of understanding. Nearly an hour after the last news, Mary arrived with a significant development: Liz might need a pacemaker with a defibrillator. It is a device that would be used to help regulate her heartbeat and potentially prevent future episodes like the ventricular fibrillation they mentioned earlier.

However, there was still a hurdle to overcome: how well Liz's brain had endured this trauma remained a mystery. Her recovery ultimately hinged on her brain activity once she awakened.

A few tense minutes later, Mary returned with another update. Liz had experienced another brief episode of ventricular fibrillation, but thankfully, her heart managed to correct itself. The doctors, in response, had started her on a beta blocker, a medication that would help regulate her heart rhythm further.

Though some clarity emerged, each new piece of information brought a fresh wave of worry. *What would the next few hours hold? Would dawn bring a twinkle of hope, or would they be facing another crisis?*

Only time would tell, and the family braced themselves, hearts heavy but spirits unbroken.

As evening cast the sky in hues of orange and purple, a difficult decision loomed. Alexis and Chris, hearts heavy with worry, knew they had to return to Beverly Hills to be with their children.

Chris drove Alexis home first. The physical distance felt immense, a cruel barrier separating them from Liz's bedside. Saying goodbye was a bitter pill to swallow, particularly for Alexis. She yearned to stay and be a pillar of strength for Emily and the others. However, priorities pulled her back, as the kids needed her back home in Beverly Hills.

After dropping off Alexis, Chris bore the weight of worry alone. He raced to Detroit Metro Airport to pick us up, the miles melting away under the urgency of his temperament.

As we settled into his car, I felt exhaustion gnawing at me.

"Let's drop our things off at home first," I suggested.

Chris shook his head, his voice barely concealing his sense of rush.

"Let's head straight to the hospital," he said.

The change in his tone sent a jolt through me. The tightness in his jaw and the apprehension flashing in his eyes. It was a subtle shift, but my gut clenched in sudden premonition.

Something was wrong—something very wrong—with my Liz. It felt as if a cold fist was squeezing my heart.

We hurried through the hospital doors, the sterile scent doing little to ease my growing nervousness. The first sight that greeted me was Mary. She had left to grab a bite but had rushed back before our arrival. One look at my worried face after the car ride and her eyes softened with deep sympathy. We didn't need words; she understood. Placing a gentle hand on my arm, she led me toward Liz's ICU room.

The heavy doors swung open, revealing a scene that stole the breath from my lungs.

Liz lay on the bed, surrounded by wires and machines. There were other faces in the room, a blur of concern, but my focus narrowed to her—my *daughter*. A pang of guilt ripped through me as I saw her pale, still form.

"So sorry, honey," I choked. "I should have been here first."

Tears flooded my eyes, blurring my vision, but I couldn't tear my gaze from her. Every fiber of my being ached to reach out, comfort her, and tell her I was finally here. Tears spilled down my face as I sank beside her bed, and a strangled sob escaped my lips. I longed to hold her and chase away the nightmare that had upended our lives.

A horrifying thought flashed through my mind: I would trade places with my beloved daughter in a heartbeat.

"It should have been me," I remember Patrick whispering similar words as he stood beside me.

This couldn't be happening. This vibrant, funny, and sarcastic girl who filled our lives with light – this couldn't be her. It felt like a harsh twist of fate, a scene ripped from a bad movie. But the machines hummed on, constantly reminding us of the unforgiving reality that had gripped us.

Denial tore at the edges of my sanity. *This couldn't be real*. My beautiful, lively daughter couldn't be reduced to this pale, still form. But as I gazed at her face, engraved with vulnerability, the truth came crashing down.

And in that moment, all I could do was hold on to the brittle hope that somehow, some way, we would get through this together.

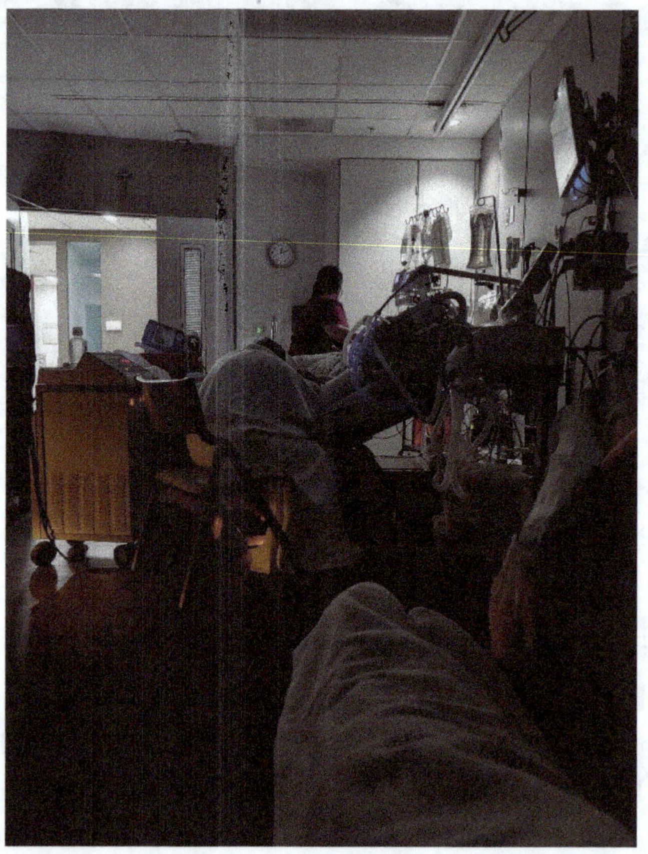

The night stretched on, each tick of the clock a blow against my fragile hope. I curled up beside Liz, clinging to her even in her sleep, as if willing her to wake with a sassy remark – "Mom, what the heck are you doing lying on top of me?"

I couldn't tear my eyes away from her, afraid that if I did, she'd just...vanish. She needed me. My daughter, *my Liz*, needed her mom. And I wasn't ready to let go.

Brimming with concern that mirrored my own, Mark carried the awful task of calling family. Each choked word he spoke seemed to tear a piece from my heart. He was speaking about my daughter from the confines of the ICU room. This whole thing felt like a nightmare we couldn't wake from. Our laughter, plans, and normal life had all been stolen away, replaced by a suffocating wave of worry.

But even in the face of that despair, something sputtered to life. Maybe it was the way Mark reached for my hand. Maybe it was the tear that escaped Patrick's eye as he squeezed my shoulder.

In that sterilized room, surrounded by machines and dread, our family bond strengthened beyond measure. This time, it wasn't built on the foundation of happy memories but on a shared struggle, a fight for the person we all loved.

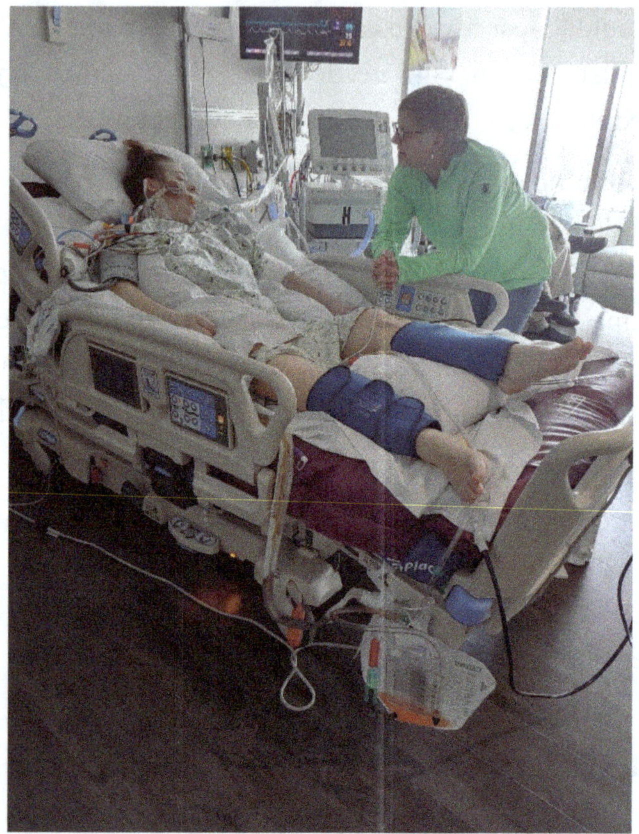

Maybe our love for her was strong enough like a tiny ember refusing to be extinguished. We gripped to that ember as the chilling grip of fear seemed to constrict us. We didn't know the future, but we knew we would face it together, one shaky step at a time.

Chapter 5: Setbacks and Strengths

The weight of that first night in the hospital pressed down on me almost physically. As I huddled beside Liz, my gaze glued to her pale face, I yearned for nothing more than to see her eyes flutter open and meet mine. Each passing moment felt like an eternity; the beeps of the machines connected to her were a relentless counterpoint to the silent scream trapped in my chest.

However, thankfully, I wasn't alone. Emily and Patrick remained by my side, spilling tears in a silent testament to our shared grief. We were a fractured family, bound together by the fragile thread of hope that stretched thin but refused to snap.

In the quiet of the night, words seemed unnecessary. A shared glance and a squeeze of a hand were small gestures that spoke volumes, a quiet promise to weather this storm together, no matter how fierce it became.

Patrick notably emerged as a pillar of strength in our collective grief, with his emotional resilience a beacon in the darkness. He knew the importance of shielding the children. Hours before Mark and I landed, he had already made the difficult journey to Emily's house with his son, Zach, by his side.

"Bailey, sweetheart," he said, "Thank you for taking such good care of the kids."

Then, his gaze shifted to the younger ones. He knelt, pulling the kids into a tight hug and explaining in a low murmur what was happening with their mother. The responsibility of protecting their children's innocence settled on his broad shoulders amidst the turmoil raging within our family.

Later that night, as we huddled around Liz's bedside, Patrick surprised me by pulling me into a gentle embrace.

"Thank you so much for coming home," he whispered. His words were a balm to the raw ache in my heart.

Tears welled up in my eyes, blurring the already indistinct image of Liz on the bed.

"Where else would I be?" I choked, my voice barely audible.

I knew Patrick was struggling with his own pain; however, he did not let that pain impact his resilience. At that moment, amidst the shared worry and fear, a realization dawned upon me: we were a family, fractured but not broken, and in the face of this crisis, our love for each other and for Liz burned bright.

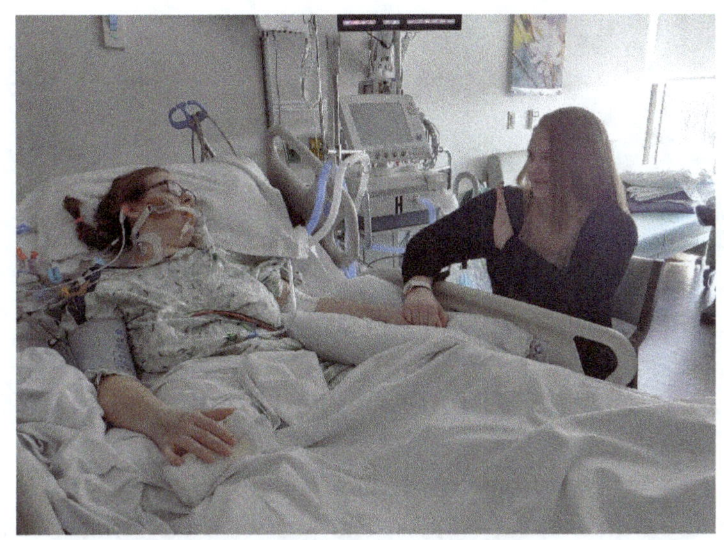

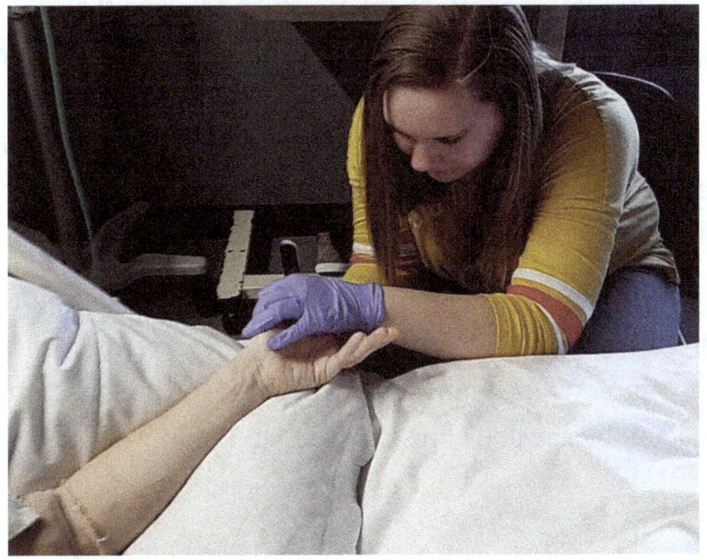

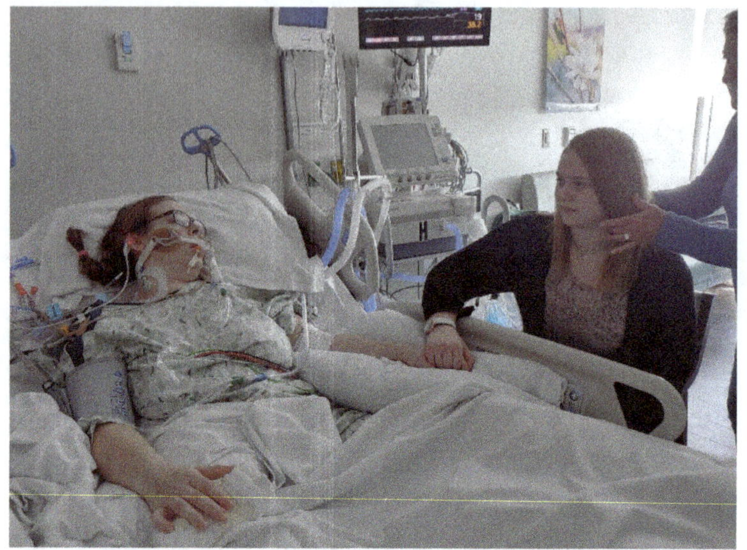

But as the night went on, keeping the truth from her own children gnawed at Emily. The past two days had been a whirlwind of confusion for Bailey and the others. They sensed the tension and the worry engraved on their mother's face, but the white lie of "everything is fine" hung heavy in the air. Bailey, however, couldn't be kept in the dark any longer, and Emily, with a heavy heart, decided to reveal the details of Liz's condition.

I understood Bailey's silent torment - a distressing ache caused by being kept in the dark and hearing reassurances that contradict the reality around you. It's a slow burn and a constant unease that chips away at your spirit.

Bailey wasn't alone in experiencing it. This crisis had ripped through our entire family, leaving a trail of emotional wreckage in its wake. It felt like a cruel thief that had stolen our laughter and normalcy and forced us to confront our vulnerability, making us rely on each other in ways we never imagined. Perhaps, in the crucible of this mutual pain, the bonds that held us together would be forged anew, stronger than ever before.

As the first rays of dawn crept through the window, casting a pale light on Liz's face, a difficult decision descended upon me. My body ached for rest, a deep sleep that now felt like a distant memory. The emotional toll of the past two days had been immense, leaving me running on fumes. But the thought of leaving Liz's side, even momentarily, sent a fresh wave of fear crashing through me.

Ultimately, it was Emily, her own eyes red-rimmed and weary, who offered a solution.

"Maybe," she suggested gently, "you could spend your days at the hospital, be there for Liz, but come home for the nights. Your body needs rest. We all do. You'll be of no use to her or yourself if you collapse from exhaustion. I'm used to the night shift, so I'll take care of the nights. Liz won't be alone, not for a moment."

Emily's words struck a chord deep within me. They weren't harsh, but their truth resonated with a dull ache; we were all at risk of crumpling under the weight of this setback. My body was a hollow shell, running on a blend of adrenaline and concern. I had to balance my need to be at Liz's bedside with the need to take care of myself.

I knew that I had to be strong for her and for all of us. I couldn't fall apart or break down. So, with a heavy heart, I nodded in agreement. It wasn't the ideal solution, but it would have to do for now.

Steadily, each day became a blur of sterile hallways and worried whispers with doctors and nurses. While exhaustion and emotional pain seemed to envelop me, I knew the doctors were doing their best to keep Liz stable. These medical professionals felt like guardian angels during the very time when our world was falling apart. They moved with a quiet purpose, and their every action and intervention was a silent promise to fight for Liz.

As I watched them work, a prayer echoed in my heart: a desperate plea for the medical professionals' knowledge and skills to be the key to Liz's recovery. I had to believe my daughter was getting the best possible care in their capable hands. It was a brittle hope, but it was all I had to cling to.

The hospital did little to offer consolation, with the rhythmic beeps of the machines in the ICU only reminding us of Liz's fragile state. Then came the doctors, with their faces engraved with a concern that mirrored the churning sensation in my gut. It couldn't be more apparent: Liz's condition was critical.

They explained she had paralysis on her right side, likely caused by strokes. These strokes, in turn, stemmed from a weak heart muscle, a condition they called cardiomyopathy. They kept mentioning the EF (ejection fraction) number, which was a mere 10–20%, a fraction of what a healthy heart should be. It meant her heart wasn't pumping blood efficiently, leaving her body starved of oxygen.

In these circumstances, the extent of the damage to her brain from the strokes remained a terrifying unknown. Each passing explanation from the doctors related to Liz's situation felt like a hammer blow or a suffocating pressure that threatened to steal my breath. But as the day progressed, a glimmer of progress emerged.

The medical team had managed to stabilize Liz by meticulously addressing imbalances in her body chemistry, those tiny building blocks that compose the balance of life. They had weaned her off sedation and believed it to be a hopeful step toward her regaining consciousness.

However, despite this improvement, a thick silence filled the air, heavy and suffocating. Liz wasn't there—not really. Her body was as beautiful as ever, but it felt like the light inside her had gone out for a while. The rhythmic beeps of the machines continued and were the only sign of life in the sterile ICU room. The doctors had discontinued most medications, leaving only a single drug called amiodarone to keep her heart rhythm steady. Amiodarone is a medication that helps control irregular heartbeats. It affects the electrical signals in the heart, like calming down a fluttering flag in a strong wind. While this drug wasn't a cure, it was a small but crucial victory in this fight for Liz's health.

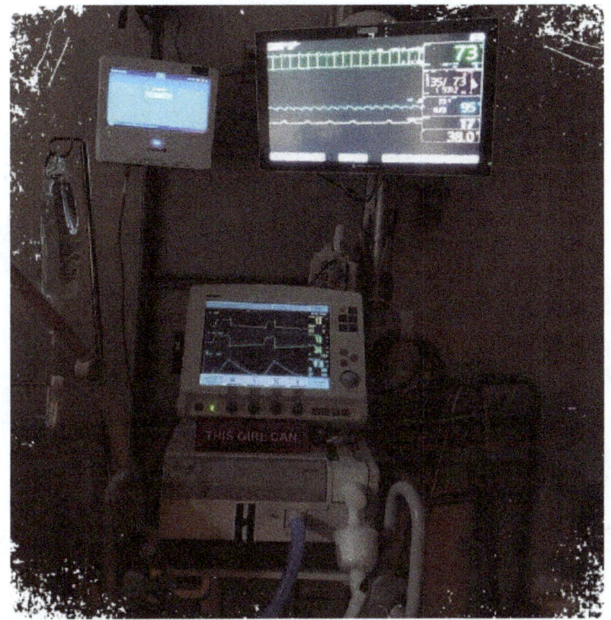

Even the slightest sign of improvement felt like a precious gift. For instance, Liz's pupils still responded to light. There were even moments of movement, though it was unclear if they were intentional or simple reflexes.

Later that night, a sliver of something more emerged. Patrick entered the room and tried to speak to Liz about the kids and how they felt about her. And then came a miracle: a slight turn of her head, a subtle response that could have been missed. But for me, it was a thunderclap in the quiet tempest.

Could it be? Was this a trace of awareness, a spark of recognition?

The tears brimming in my eyes were equal parts relief and hope, a desperate desire that this tiny movement was a sign of progress, a promise of the daughter I knew returning to me at long last.

Emily arrived later that day, and with a playful glint in her eye, she tickled Liz's foot, and to her amazement, Liz recoiled! She was aware of and registering stimuli. This wasn't just a random reflex— Liz was fighting back.

This newfound awareness extended even to the discomfort of medical procedures. When the nurses came to suction her airway, a frown creased her brow, and she instinctively turned away.

The EEG, a test that measured her brain activity, had been scheduled for the following Monday. However, in light of these subtle improvements, they decided to delay it. Perhaps, they reasoned, giving her more time to recover would provide a clearer picture of the damage the strokes had inflicted.

It was another agonizing wait for me, but this time, it was tinged with a trace of hope. Liz was showing signs, however faint, of clawing her way back to stability. And that, for now, was all that mattered.

There were still hurdles to overcome, of course. The doctors updated me on her internal functions: her kidneys were functioning well, a positive sign. However, her liver enzymes were elevated, which they explained could be a side effect of the medications she was on. These drugs, necessary to keep her comfortable and sedated, could take longer to leave her system due to her liver's temporary strain. It was a technical explanation, but the underlying message was clear: her body was working hard to fight on multiple fronts.

Although the medical jargon seemed to overwhelm me, the sentiment resonated deeply. Liz was a fighter, that much I knew. In fact, Emily mentioned she had never tolerated narcotics well, and even with her medication, she marched to the beat of her own drum. She further explained that Liz would likely clear them from her system at her own pace. Liz never did anything by the book.

And perhaps, in this instance, her stubborn independence was exactly what she needed. It was a small detail and a quirk in her medical profile, but at that moment, it felt like a tiny spark of her personality was returning. And that, more than anything, filled me with a renewed sense of hope, and consequently, a fierce resolve took root within me.

I wouldn't give up on Liz. Not now, not *ever*.

In the face of this emotional upheaval, the untiring comfort of our loved ones became a crucial source of support.

We were incredibly grateful for the outpouring of love from friends and family. However, Liz's fragile state demanded a carefully managed environment.

With her neurological condition still unclear, the constant stream of doctors in and out of the ICU became a chaotic ballet. To allow her brain the best chance to heal, we had to limit visitors and stimulation to a minimum. Even phone calls and texts from family, though heartfelt, were restricted.

It was a difficult decision, but her well-being was paramount.

The constant hum of activity outside her sterile room starkly contrasted with the calm we sought within. Yet, amidst the controlled chaos, the love and concern pouring in from afar resonated deeply. It was a powerful reminder that we weren't alone in this fight. Rather, we were surrounded by an invisible army of love, and that knowledge drove my willpower to see Liz through this.

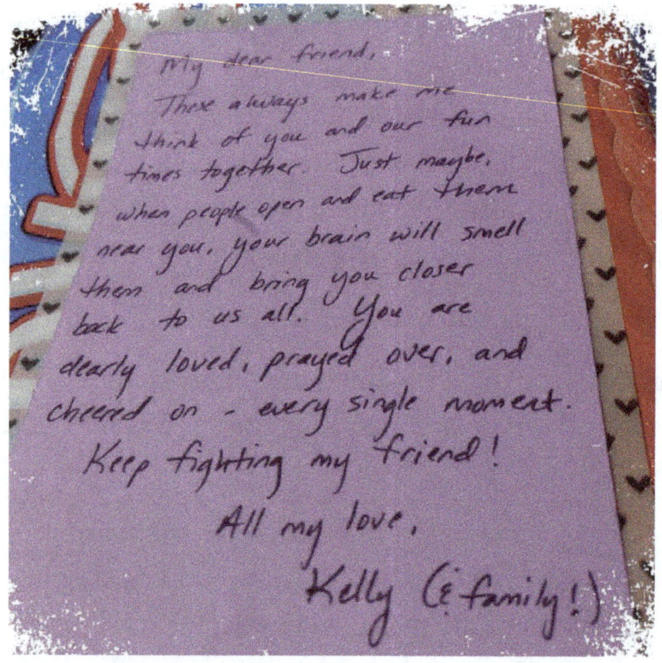

On days when our endurance was constantly being tested due to the updates on Liz's condition, our large extended family appeared like a beacon of warmth piercing through the fog. They noticed the toll this ordeal was taking upon us and rallied around us - not with their physical presence in those uncertain COVID times, but with a different kind of support: the gift of nourishing meals delivered to our doorstep.

It was a simple act but a kindness that went straight to the heart. It was a tangible expression of their love. And so, the invisible army that surrounded us took on a more concrete form that nourished our bodies and spirits.

Fortunately, this love extended far beyond the confines of our area. The support we received wasn't limited to those in our immediate vicinity. This brings to mind my dearest friend, Rema, who lives in Saskatchewan, Canada, and could not visit due to COVID-19 restrictions. Instead, she chose to send an email expressing her immense love and support.

Kathy!!

How often you are in my thoughts! Not wanting to burden you with correspondence you will feel obligated to deal with, I have hesitated in writing - if you need a shoulder or ear, please call me anytime. I'm sure a break from what has become normal might be welcome but may also feel irreverent... You might feel guilty for doing "for-Kathy" - swimming, a nap, a glass of vino tinto, laughing at anything... I don't know what I'm talking about really. I try to put myself in your position; there's a protective wall that won't let a mom fully immerse in that horror. I'm sure all of your friends would say the same. I hate that Liz is where she is, and I despise that you are challenged in this way. I don't know anyone else who can deal like you can or a man like Mark who can support like he does - really! The recent public health issues must be the last straw. My plan was to visit you when the right time came, pull you out of your head and talk about nonsense, have a drink or 'philosophize,' and pray and cry - whatever is necessary. That won't happen for a good long while with travel restrictions and social distancing enforced. When travel is allowed, distance be damned. I hope only that my prayers for Liz and you are answered.

Here, we are self-quarantining x 10'ish more days, haven't seen my babies exc by FT, but we have our health! Doing needlework, cleaning, yoga and, going for walks, power-watching "Downton Abbey," playing cards to stay busy. We were looking forward to seeing other ppl after "just us" in HUX, but alas, it's just us for a while more - we are fortunate that we can laugh together. We haven't visited our moms yet either but this too shall pass. They are well. Very wintery here, but spring will be welcome for many reasons! Dan sends a hug and his love-

You are a wonderful mom, Kathy. Maybe your other identities will be good 'distractions' at times now, esp when your visits to Liz are restricted. God bless you, dear girl. Rema (PS no reply necessary)

Not only did my friends offer their encouragement through written words, but a friend of Mary's, Sarah, also conveyed her love and checked in on us through a heartfelt letter:

Liz,

It's been years since I've seen you, but Mary has been keeping me informed of your progress. I have been praying for you multiple times every day, thinking about you, and hoping for a full recovery. You're on my mind constantly. What a blessing to have such an incredible family surrounding you. I'll continue to keep tabs on you through Mary. Will be cheering you on from Alabama! You've got this.

In addition, friends like Scott and Leah, though miles away in Canada, reached out in a powerful wave of support. Their steadfast presence, even from afar, was a demonstration of the enduring strength of friendship. Prayers were said for Liz and for us—a collective outpouring of hope that resonated across continents.

It was then that news reached me: church masses were being held in Liz's honor. Tears of relief and gratitude welled up in my eyes. Amid our quiet, desperate struggle, it felt like a lifeline thrown from the heavens. Someone, somewhere, knew of our suffering, and they were offering their prayers and well wishes for my precious Liz. The distance between us melted away, replaced by a powerful bond of shared hope. At that moment, I felt a surge of strength and a renewed belief that we could battle this chaos. God was working through these kind strangers, offering comfort and hope in our darkest hour.

Among these were our dear friends, Leslie and Andy, who reached out with a gift: a Bible. The Holy Book appeared like a roadmap through the deceitful terrain we were navigating. They had meticulously outlined passages and verses filled with strength, consolation, and the power of faith. As I devoured those words, they persistently reminded us that we were not unaccompanied but watched over by a Higher Power.

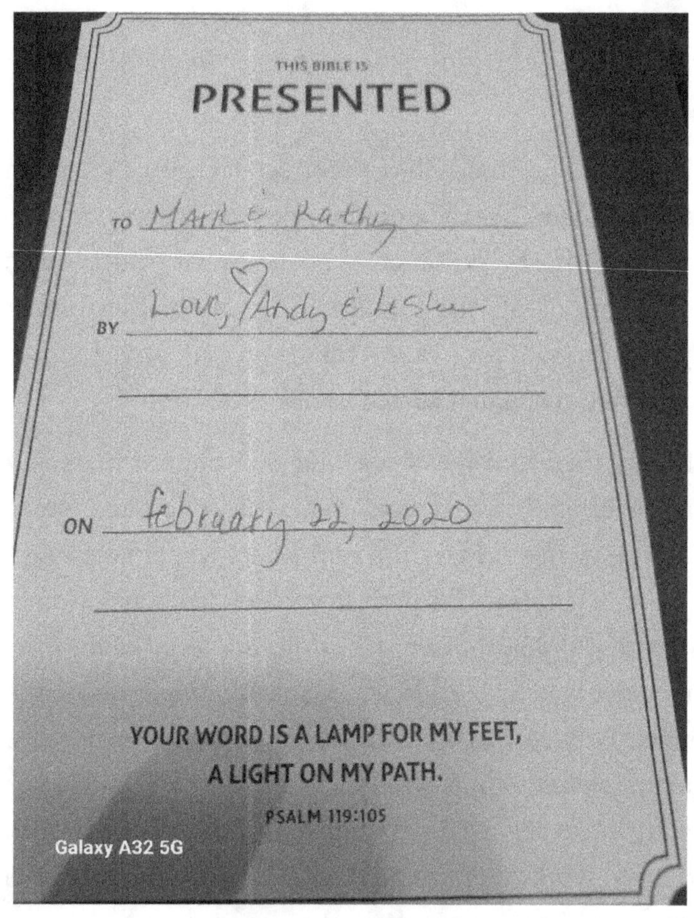

Faith, I came to realize, wasn't about blind acceptance but about holding on to hope in the face of uncertainty. It was the hand reaching out to steady me when the ground beneath my feet seemed to crumble. Faith became my shield in the quiet vigils by Liz's bedside amidst the whirring of machines. It wasn't a magic cure but a source of strength and a wellspring of optimism that I could draw from.

In those moments when despair threatened to consume me, we chose to turn to prayer and supplication. It gave us a sense of peace, a way to release our fears and worries. We believed that God had a plan, even if we didn't understand it then. Trusting in His wisdom helped us find the courage to face each new trial.

Every new update from the medical team brimmed us with hope that perhaps today would be the day Liz would take another step toward recovery. With faith as our compass and the support of our loved ones as our guide, we were prepared to walk this path with her.

"So do not fear, for I am with you; do not be dismayed, for I am your God. I will strengthen you and help you; I will uphold you with my righteous right hand."

-Isaiah 41:10

Chapter 6: Glimmers of Recovery

The week had stretched like an eternity, a relentless tide of worry and exhaustion each day. By Monday, the neurologist's words hung heavy in the air, a dark cloud threatening to drown out all hope. Gary, Mark, Emily, Mary, and I had taken turns holding vigil at Liz's bedside, a silent huddle against the encroaching turmoil.

During that period, sleep was a fleeting luxury, stolen briefly between hushed updates from the doctors. But through it all, a single, fierce determination burned within us: we wouldn't give up on Liz.

Tuesday morning arrived, and Patrick and I, along with Mark and Christopher, were ushered into a small conference room. The air crackled with a tension that mirrored the knot of worry tightening in my stomach. Doctors and staff awaited us, their faces stamped with a seriousness that sent shivers down my spine.

A pile of medical images lay on the table, and I knew, with a sickening certainty, that this meeting would determine Liz's fate. Taking a deep breath, I steeled myself.

"We see evidence of two large strokes and four smaller ones," the neurologist began, "They're located on the left side of the brain, which explains the paralysis on Liz's right side."

A glimmer of hope arose within me: paralysis could be managed, and rehabilitation was possible. But then, his next words snuffed out that fragile spark.

"However, the brainstem appears to be relatively affected."

My heart sank. In my limited medical knowledge, the brainstem meant control of vital functions.

"I know what I would do," he finished, his gaze lingering on the images.

The implication hung heavy in the air; there was little hope for recovery. Meanwhile, a cold fury rumbled within me. *Three days*? Liz was only 38 years old. This wasn't supposed to happen to someone so young, someone with her whole life ahead of her. The doctor's words sounded like a dark pronouncement that defied logic.

Didn't they see the fight in Liz's eyes, even if they were closed? They spoke with such clinical detachment, a recitation of medical facts that stripped away any trace of hope. Their somber expressions felt almost performative, a charade of empathy that did little to ease the crushing weight of their prognosis. It felt like they were already mourning Liz, whispering goodbyes while she still clung to life.

This wasn't the kind of support we needed. We needed fighters in Liz's corner, not doctors who seemed to have already surrendered.

At that moment, I couldn't help but wonder about this doctor's faith in his patient's ability to heal. This so-called "Doctor Doom," as I silently christened him, offered a prognosis based on statistics, not on the indomitable spirit I knew resided within my daughter.

Just then, a nurse chimed in. "If we disconnect Liz from life support..." she trailed off, but we knew what her words implied. My fists clenched involuntarily, the urge to lash out a primal reaction I fought to contain.

Patrick rose abruptly and left the room. As soon as the door closed behind him, a sob escaped my lips. Tears streamed down my face in a mixture of grief, frustration, and a fierce, untiring love for Liz.

We wouldn't let this doctor, this defeatist attitude, define her future. Liz was in this fight, and so were we. Every fiber of my being rebelled against the notion of giving up.

Two days later, a beacon of light pierced the oppressive gloom. Elizabeth, Liz's stepsister, arrived. She had driven from Detroit without hesitation, demonstrating the concrete bond our family shared. Packed and ready for action, she met Mark at a shoe store. High tops, they explained, were needed to prevent a complication called "drop foot." The scene felt almost surreal—a desperate scramble for normalcy amidst the crushing gravity of our situation.

We were all fumbling through the darkness, holding on to any semblance of routine to maintain our sanity. After the quick shopping trip, they drove separately to the hospital, each car carrying a silent prayer for Liz's recovery.

Arriving at the hospital, Elizabeth entered the room, bringing a much-needed breath of fresh air. Gary, Patrick, and I sat huddled around Liz's bed in a silent vigil against the tribulation we were confronted with. Elizabeth's presence reminded us that we weren't alone in this fight.

The visit, however, was a grueling one. Liz remained on the ventilator, a tangle of tubes and machines that masked the vibrant woman we knew.

Meanwhile, Gary knelt beside Liz, holding her hand and whispering words of love and encouragement. Yet, the usually steady strength in his voice faltered, a crack betraying the raw emotion churning beneath the surface.

"Come on, sweetheart, you can fight this. You're strong, Liz. Don't give up," he murmured.

The sight of Gary was an unadulterated reminder of the toll this ordeal was taking on all of us.

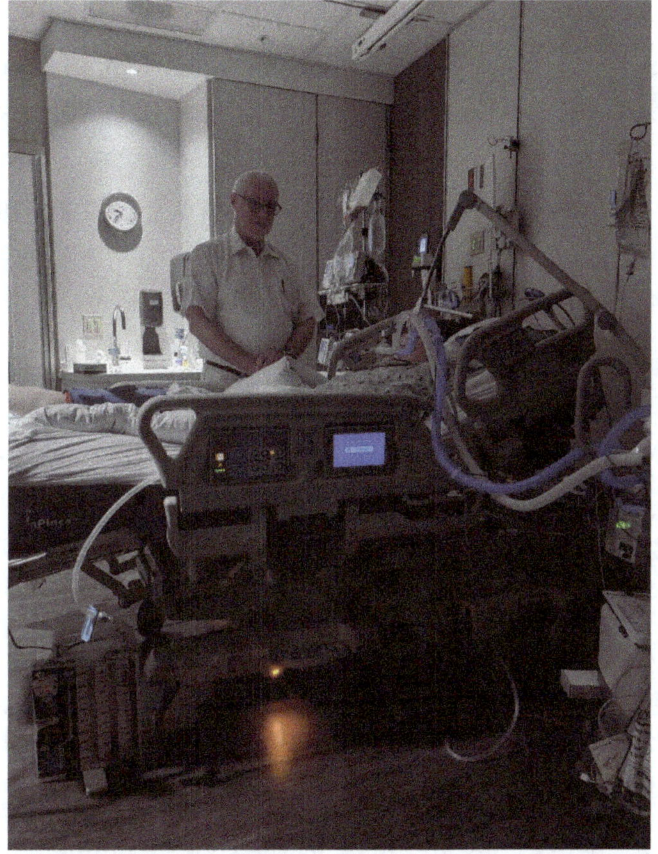

Back in Beverly Hills, Alexis, separated from Liz by miles and circumstance, felt the passage of time warp. The week since Chris had brought her home stretched before her like a wearying month. He himself had returned for a few days that week before rejoining us at the hospital, and Alexis, thankfully, was able to follow suit a few days later.

Then, a whisper of hope—a gentle breeze came rustling through the barren branches of despair. Liz began to show the tiniest hint of progress. Her previously vacant eyes now seemed to fixate on a single point, tracking the voice that addressed her. It wasn't much; a blink or a slight turn of the head—but a fragile connection bloomed in that moment. When Chris entered the room, her gaze seemed to seek him out, a silent recognition that warmed our hearts. She wasn't speaking, but the subtle shift in her awareness was a pinprick of light piercing the overpowering darkness. She flinched at pain, a response that grounded us in a reality both hopeful and heartbreaking. These were baby steps, agonizingly slow, but each one depicted Liz's indomitable spirit.

We gripped these tiny victories, driving our willpower to see her through this strenuous fight. Each fragment of progress and each tentative step forward fired our fortitude. A new sense of purpose thrived within us, a shared mission to help Liz reclaim her life.

It was during that visit that Elizabeth took a leap of faith. With a hesitant smile, she reached out and grasped Liz's hand.

Elizabeth's voice trembled as she spoke. "I think... I think she's in there," she whispered, her gaze locked on mine.

Tears brimmed in my eyes, clouding my vision.

"I think you're right," I choked back a sob, a single word resounding the truth that gushed in our hearts.

We knew that Liz was fighting her way back to stability.

As Mark and Elizabeth left for the house, the weight of the day settled on us. They were unsure whether to cry or take a short rest, with neither option holding a clear answer for them. The gathering in the kitchen at home later that evening stayed etched in their minds. A somber mood hung heavily in the air, a collective sigh after the emotional rollercoaster.

Then, a spark: a shared joke, a memory of Liz, and a burst of laughter erupted, shattering the tense silence.

The laughter, however, felt laced with a touch of guilt, quickly smothered by the returning weight of worry. The pendulum swung back and forth: grief, humor, and a desperate search for normalcy amidst the grief. It was a raw, emotional display and clearly portrayed the powerful bond holding us together.

Yet, in the face of impossible odds, we found strength in each other, a glimmer of courage rekindled by Liz's tiny victories.

As Elizabeth closed her eyes that night, a single, fragile thought surfaced in her mind. It wasn't a grand declaration or a burst of sunshine; rather, it was a whisper, a tiny seed of confidence taking root in the fertile ground of her love for Liz. Exhaustion tugged at her limbs, the emotional toll of the day a heavy weight on her shoulders.

Though, beneath the fatigue, a quiet resolve hummed. Liz was tearing her way back from the darkness, a slow, excruciating process but a process nonetheless. Each spasm of a finger and each time she held a slight recognition in her eyes felt like a victory hard-won. It represented her strength and silent insubordination against the odds and medical pronouncements stacked against her.

It was a promise inscribed onto our hearts that we would be there for Liz every step of the way. The struggle was far from over, but a shared resolution throbbed through us, guiding our actions.

During those crucial days, another glimmer of clarity emerged, this time providing a better understanding of our situation. Andrea, my niece, a brilliant neurologist, arrived for a visit. Her medical assessment, while cautious, held a spark of encouragement.

"She needs time," she said. "It's a long road, but there are signs of progress."

Those words were a decisive source of support, appearing as the first tentative step onto solid ground after days floating at sea. A wave of relief washed over me, a physical sensation that loosened the bulge of tension in my chest. Liz might not be the same, the path to recovery shrouded in ambiguity, but one thing was clear: *she was coming back to us.*

The unknown loomed large, a vast and unfamiliar territory. How much function would she regain? What would her new normal look like? Would she ever walk again? Talk again? *Live independently?* The questions scraped at me, and the future stretched before us. It was a scary thought, one that sent shivers down my spine. However, a quiet sense of gratitude bloomed within me for the first time since Liz fell ill.

Liz was alive and making progress. And that, in that moment, was all that mattered.

This fragile hope was tested anew when the latest update arrived. Liz had developed a fever, a worrying sign that signaled the presence of an infection. Fevers, in a patient like Liz, could complicate her recovery, acting like a roadblock on her already arduous journey. The doctors would need to act swiftly to identify the source of the infection and treat it aggressively.

Another piece of news, though seemingly minor, sent a fresh wave of worry crashing over me. Liz was exhibiting movement in her left arm, even attempting to grab at her face. While a positive development in itself, it also presented a challenge. The nurses, out of an abundance of caution, had opted to restrain her arm loosely to prevent any potential self-inflicted injuries during the night. It was a necessary step, but the image of Liz, even partially restrained, filled me with a pang of sadness.

The rollercoaster of emotions continued, with flimsy anticipation battling against the ever-present undercurrent of fear. Each update brought a mix of relief and anxiety, making it hard to find steady emotional ground. We navigated these furious waters as best as we could, clinging to every bit of progress while bracing ourselves for the unknown.

Chris stayed with Liz during the weekend to give Emily a break, but she would return for the next few days until she needed to go back to work. We accepted this as the new normal for a while, supporting Patrick and the kids as much as we could. It wasn't easy; every day felt like walking a tightrope, hopeful for progress yet bracing for setbacks. There were nights when the hospital felt cold and unwelcoming, contrasting blatantly with the warmth of our usual family routine. But we were there for each other, sharing smiles during good news and holding each other tight during the tough times. The kids were troopers, adapting to this new reality with surprising resilience.

We all held on to the hope that Liz would recover and that laughter would once again fill our home.

With a glimmer of hope, the doctors planned to extubate Liz mid-week. This meant carefully removing the breathing tube and seeing if she could breathe adequately on her own. It was a nervous time for everyone, as it was unclear how Liz would respond. *Would her lungs be strong enough after being on the ventilator for so long?*

We didn't know if she could sustain breathing on her own. Normally, the diaphragm, the main muscle for breathing, contracts and relaxes to draw air into the lungs. When someone is on a ventilator for a long time, their diaphragm muscles can become weak. This can make it difficult to breathe on their own, especially when they're first taken off the ventilator. Their lungs, unused to working so hard, might struggle.

Thankfully, the nursing care has been amazing. They were the ones who constantly monitored Liz and made sure she was comfortable. They were also there to help us understand the medical jargon and answer any questions we had. Their expertise and compassion were a major source of comfort during this crisis.

Upon reflection, this experience has undoubtedly made us appreciate the people around us more. Friends and family have been there for us with their overwhelming love and support. A simple phone call, a dropped-off meal, or even just a listening ear has meant the world. It serves as a reminder that we don't face challenges alone, and the love of those around us can be a powerful source of strength.

To this day, we are incredibly grateful for every one of them.

Chapter 7: Long Road to Rehabilitation

Two weeks crawled by in the ICU, each day bringing a trace of hope with new movements on Liz's left side and then the right. We would watch, hearts pounding, as her fingers twitched or her toes curled.

Even more encouragingly, she tried to cough, and there was some head and jaw movement. It wasn't much, but these small signs felt like significant progress in the face of uncertainty and were a major source of reassurance that she was still fighting.

But then came the setbacks, one after another, like punches to the gut. Her lung collapsed, forcing doctors to insert a chest tube into her lung. While this was a scary development, it ensured she got the needed oxygen, and her lungs were being reinflated.

A few days later, she needed a feeding tube, a relentless reminder of her current limitations but also a comforting sign that her body was still receiving the essential nutrients to fight.

Then came the news of a blood clot in her arm at an old IV site. On top of everything else, this complication was a heavy blow when the neurologist's report came in. Despite her tiny improvements, the overall picture was far from positive. A fresh wave of despair washed over us.

Were these small movements all we could hope for? The fight suddenly felt heavier, and the path forward seemed less clear. And so, we held on to each other as we had until then, lost and afraid in the face of profuse uncertainty.

Every new answer seemed to bring more questions; every step forward felt met with two steps back. To make matters even more confusing, Liz's MRI was canceled and not rescheduled. We were left in the dark, grasping for any explanation.

Here, a glimmer of assurance emerged in the form of Dr. Bennett, who had performed Liz's hysterectomy just a week ago and stepped in as her doctor and friend. He spoke with Dr. Farooq, a specialist in stroke management, and informed us that Dr. Farooq would be reviewing the initial MRI. This progression felt like a major improvement in Liz's situation. Perhaps Dr. Farooq could see something we couldn't—a path forward out of this confusing maze.

Steadily, Liz began to progress with her motor skills and communication. She slowly began tracking us with her eyes, a silent conversation budding in the sterilized room. After a while, the question we had all been waiting for came: a mouthing of words, a silent plea for answers.

One day, her eyes met mine, and she mouthed a question that shattered the silence of the ICU room: *"What happened?"* It was a simple phrase, but for me, it felt like a beacon in the darkness. Here she was, finally asking, and I poured out everything that had happened, my voice trembling slightly. She was clearly confused and lost in a situation she didn't understand. But all I could do was hold her hand, a silent promise to be there through everything, a steady presence amid ambiguity.

As the days went by, she continued to ask the same question, *"What happened?"* Each time, I patiently answered, knowing that her mind was grappling with the enormity of the situation. It was as if she was trying to piece together a puzzle that kept slipping from her grasp. Each question reminded me of the fragile state she was in, but it was also an opportunity for me to reaffirm my commitment to being by her side, no matter how many times it took to help her find the answers she sought.

In those moments, with the tracheostomy tube in place, a strange sense of relief took over me, and we could see her more clearly. It was a different kind of vulnerability, but somehow, my Liz felt more like herself. Despite the new tube, she still exuded a quiet beauty, a strength that mirrored her former self. It was then we noticed she had bitten the front of her tongue. It wasn't a new injury but a sign of the struggle she had been through, a sheer portrayal of her endurance to pain and her battle to survive.

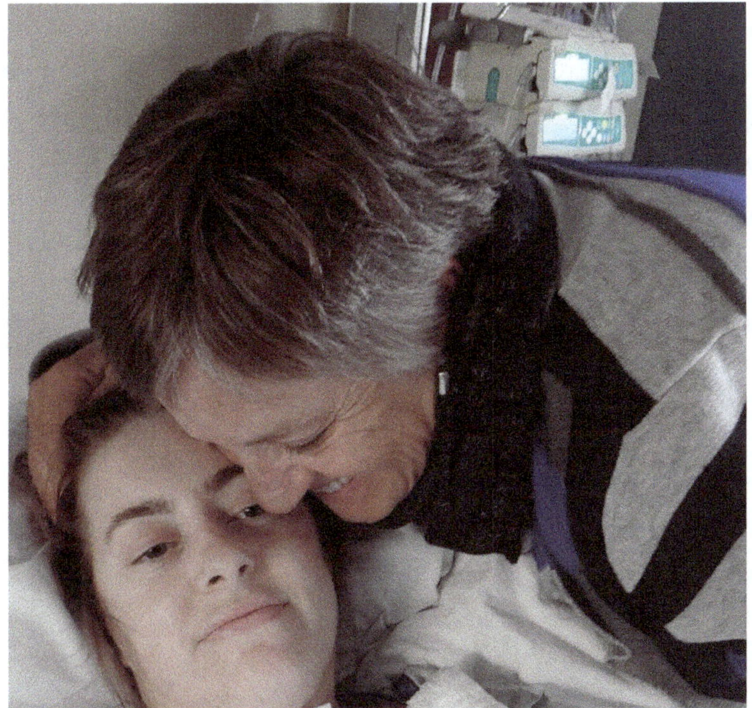

Liz's struggle to improve spoke volumes about her inner strength, inspiring us to keep fighting alongside her. Every minor movement and response to a voice filled us with renewed hope. She opened her eyes more readily, focusing on whoever was in the room. But the most reassuring sign after removing the breathing tube was the movement of her lips. Liz was healing-recovering from the multiple strokes. And then, one day, a miracle happened: *she smiled!*

For the first time in days, Liz's pale, lifeless face was replaced by someone I vividly remembered. It felt like the sun breaking through the clouds, a moment of celebration. It was the most beautiful sight we could have imagined, a tiny spark of her personality returning to the surface.

While we were savoring these precious moments as a family, we were also keenly aware of the many people who cared about Liz. Distant relatives and friends, all eager to offer their support, wanted to visit and sit with us.

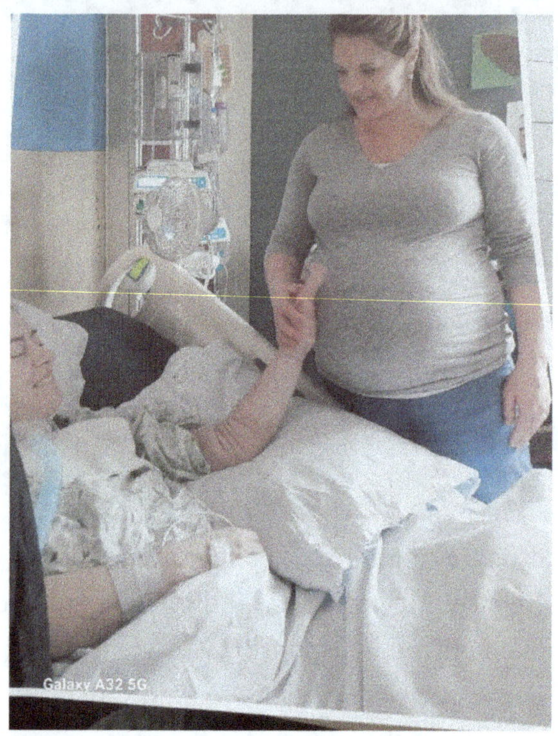

Their kindness and well wishes were a source of strength, constantly reminding us that we were not isolated in our challenging times. But there were days when I needed Liz to myself. The constant stream of visitors, some of whom she barely knew, felt overwhelming. It wasn't that I didn't appreciate their love; it just felt like much at times.

Understandably, Patrick felt the same way. He wanted Liz to heal at her own pace, to focus on getting stronger without the added stress of unfamiliar faces. While well-meaning, every ounce of her energy was precious, and visitors could be draining. He yearned for the day Liz would return to her usual self—when laughter would fill the room again. But for now, he believed her privacy was paramount.

After all, she was in the ICU, in a vulnerable state, a million miles away from the strong, vibrant woman she usually was. We both felt strongly that she wouldn't have wanted to be seen like that by people she wasn't close to. It was hard to imagine explaining her condition to everyone who wanted to visit. We wanted her to heal with some dignity, on her own terms, and not have to put on a brave face for visitors.

Consequently, we confided in the ICU staff, asking them to gently redirect visitors who lingered too long. Perhaps it felt a little extreme, but I guarded her privacy in those moments. These unanticipated visits, while well-intentioned, felt like an intrusion on her fragile recovery.

Liz was my daughter, not a museum exhibit put on display. At that particular time, all I craved was some privacy and a quiet space for our family to reconcile with these challenging circumstances together.

And maybe, when Liz was stronger, we could open the doors a bit wider. We could share her progress with loved ones, celebrate her victories, and maybe even laugh together again. But for now, our focus was solely on Liz—on helping her rebuild her strength, one precious, weak smile at a time.

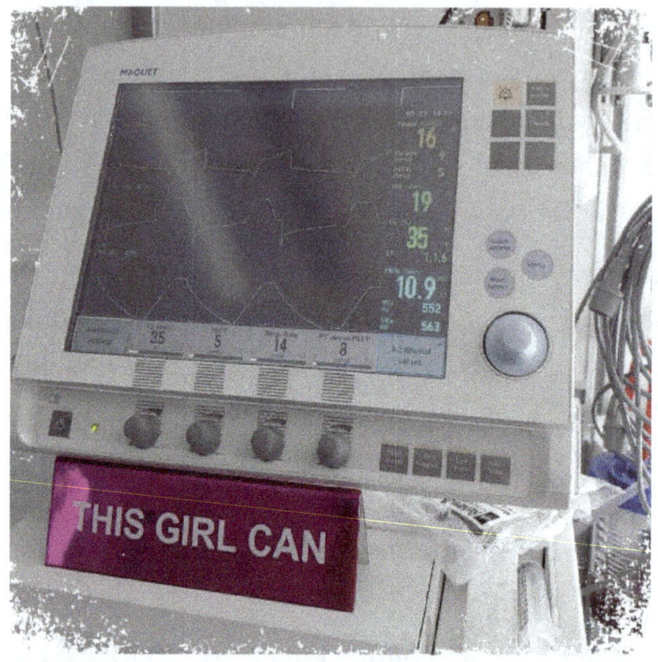

It was a slow, painstaking process, a series of tiny victories strung together one by one, where every day felt like a battle. However, every trace of progress powered my willpower to keep her close to me and not give up on her. There was comfort in her presence, even in her weakened state, surrounded by machines and beeps.

After two long weeks in the ICU, the doctors finally felt confident enough to move Liz to a step-down unit. It was a huge relief, a turning point that felt like a victory lap after a grueling marathon. This new unit was part of the Mercy Hospital network, a familiar environment where they would focus on getting Liz off the ventilator and removing her tracheostomy tube. These were big hurdles to overcome, but our confidence in Liz's recovery shone a little brighter with each step forward.

Navigating the path to rehab wasn't as straightforward as we had hoped. We felt the clinical coordinator wasn't moving as quickly as we believed necessary for Liz's case.

This was a frustrating time for everyone involved. We had finally found a sense of stability, and these new suggestions felt like a step backward. Our primary concern was ensuring Liz received the best possible care in a nearby facility where she wouldn't feel isolated.

However, the clinical coordinator's approach appeared distant, uncaring, and unhelpful. It is possible that her reluctance to approach or communicate with Liz was due to concerns about COVID-19. However, her demeanor came across as impersonal and clinical. Unlike the coordinator, no other staff members showed hesitation in interacting with Liz.

Ultimately, with some persistence on our part, we were able to secure Liz a place at Mary Free Bed Rehabilitation in Grand Rapids, Michigan. Located approximately 35 miles from home, this critically acclaimed facility offered the ideal environment for her recovery. It was a decision we made as a family, with my sister Jill playing a vital role in advocating for Liz's needs and securing her a spot at this prestigious rehab center.

Jill had been a constant source of support and strength since she learned about Liz's condition. Just three days after

Liz's cardiac arrest, Jill, along with Karen and Ron, were by our side. The moment Jill entered Liz's hospital room, the atmosphere shifted. Her eyes filled with tears as she gently caressed Liz's face, her hands tracing the contours of her niece's features. It was a heartbreaking yet beautiful display of love and resilience.

In the days that followed, Jill became our lifeline. Her emails, filled with encouragement and practical advice, provided an invaluable source of support. She checked in regularly, inquiring about Liz's progress and offering to help however she could.

For me, particularly, her support and words of reassurance made a significant difference. They empowered me, reminding me of my inner strength and resilience. In those challenging moments, Jill's belief in my ability to navigate this ordeal inspired me.

Moreover, she profoundly conveyed the power of family and community through her writings. She shared stories of how she, Tommy, and Kristen found solace in prayer at the Danny Thomas Pavilion at St. Jude's. Their collective prayers and well wishes from friends and family created a supportive network that enveloped us all. It was a reminder that during our difficult moments, a community of love and support surrounded us. This realization brought peace and comfort, a quiet strength that helped us endure the challenges ahead.

Kathy,

I am pasting the info I sent my kids—just to update you:

Karen, Ron, and I went to Muskegon today to see Liz. It's hard to explain it all, but we are so glad we were there.

There were so many tears, hugs, and expressions of love. They are all devastated by this situation. We got to spend some time with Liz. She is not awake, but I could hold her hand, touch her feet, stroke her hair, and tell her how much I love her.

The CT scan showed today that she had six strokes on one side of her brain. The neurologist who spoke to the family said that if she survives, she will be paralyzed on the right side of her body. The EEG shows brain activity—not as much as they hoped, but there is some activity.

When I was in there, Patrick was talking to her and said, "She just squeezed my hand." The priest who married Kathy and Mark came and told me that when he walked in, Liz opened her eyes almost fully and then closed them.

As Patrick said today, "We got some bad news, but we had some good things happen too."

Liz looks beautiful—and that sounds weird to say, but she does. Her color is amazing, and she looks so calm. We know the Liz we knew may not be coming back as she was; we just hope she returns with enough of her abilities to have a good life with a husband and family who will be there to help her in any way they can. Patrick is amazing and is holding down the fort with the kids, staying as strong as he can.

They are not sure of everything—apparently, she has cardiomyopathy and an enlarged heart. The cardiologist said that she must have had this for some time. Patrick told Dad she had some heart issues while living in Indy but was told she was okay. Who knows? None of this is clear. There are lots of upset people trying to piece together the picture. Apparently, Emily has something with her heart, too; I only heard that tonight and don't know what it is.

The surgeon who operated on her was there today. He was crying when he saw her. The cardiologist assured him that this was not due to the surgery but rather due to underlying heart issues.

There isn't much more to say at this point. Her heart looks good, and the cardiologist is pleased with her progress and function—she has been stable in that department for some time.

We hugged, cried, and comforted each other, knowing there was a tough road ahead for this family. They know we are there when they need us. There is so little we can do but love them at this point. They are hopeful but realistic. It will be a day-by-day process from here on.

Patty—call me in the morning. I am headed to bed soon, exhausted from all this. I can update you on the food, etc.

Love you all,

Jill.

In fact, Jill's untiring support extended beyond her initial visit. Days later, she shared an unexpected development. A conversation with a friend, a member of her book club, had opened new doors for Liz's recovery. Jane, a key figure at Mary Free Bed, had offered to evaluate Liz for a specialized rehabilitation program. According to Jane, this program was designed for patients with complex needs, offering state-of-the-art equipment and a team of highly skilled clinicians. It was an opportunity too good to pass up, as Jill forwarded Jane's email, giving us the details and encouraging us to consider this next step in Liz's recovery.

Dear Kathy and Emily,

After I left Kathy's last night and took Karen back to her car, I had to decide to attend book club. I really did not want to go, but it is my group of close friends, and Leslie had prepared a lovely meal and made an effort, so I went.

At the end of the dinner, I shared Liz's story. None of these friends knew about this, as I have not told anyone; it really was too hard to talk about. We all prayed. Jane, who "runs" so much of Mary Free Bed, jumped right in to offer her help. She has seen miracles and really believes that they can make a difference for Liz. She offered to reach out and help in the process of evaluation IF IT IS WANTED by the family. They evaluate Liz and see if she is a good candidate. Jane said the sooner she starts rehab, the greater the recovery. She said Mary Free Bed offers the most equipment and the best clinicians in the country and will give Liz an excellent chance. If she is a candidate, they do all the work to get her admission and insurance approval.

So, I am forwarding the email she sent to me last night. This is your business, and I do not mean to intervene, but I wanted you to know what she said and how she and others can help.

I do not know if we will hear from Holly via email or if we will reach out to her, but if you want, I can call her, or you can call her. Talk about it and let me know if you want me to contact her, but the family is the one who has to ask for the evaluation. Or tell me to just leave things alone at this point. Just wanted you to know this information and know if I can help in any way, let me know.

Jane is a very bright and caring person, and she will help in any way if asked to. She can answer any questions you may have as well.

Love you

As is apparent in this message, Jill's proactive nature was a light of hope during this challenging time. Her suggestion to explore specialized rehabilitation options at Mary Free Bed opened new doors for Liz's recovery, and we were eager to learn more about this potential path forward.

After careful consideration, Mary suggested we contact Holly to get more information and initiate the evaluation process. While we understood that this was just the first step, a potential pathway to even more advanced care for Liz, the complications and chaos at the hospital seemed to delay the move. Upon voicing my concerns to Jill, she emailed Emily, encouraging us to take the first step so Liz could be introduced to PT and therapy sooner.

Emily,

Sounds like things are going well. I don't know if you talked to Patrick about MFB, but I would love to encourage him to at least get the referral asked for - he can call Holly directly and do it if he wants to ask questions. Or you can help him with that. It does not commit Liz to admission, but they will evaluate her (which may take some time), and they will know when she is ready to go. They offer medical support, too.

At least the process would be started. From all I know, the sooner they can start PT and therapy on Liz, the better the recovery will be. They will assess when she is ready. They won't push it sooner. With you leaving this week, it would be great by then if the assessment was at least requested so things can get in motion. I do believe this will make a difference for Liz, but I don't want to be pushy; I just want to help. I can do anything you need me to do. Jane and Holly are great resources, and I think they will really help you when the time comes. They deal with all the insurance, too!

Please let me know if you need anything. (or if I should back off). Didn't want to bug your mom about this, but I know you are very involved in Liz's care. Love you much.

Jill

After we were provided clarity on the process and ensured that it was going in the right direction, we grew optimistic that Liz could begin her recovery journey soon, surrounded by familiar faces and a supportive environment. It was a fresh start, a chance for Liz to rebuild her strength and slowly return to the life she loved.

Looking back, I realize I must have come across as demanding, maybe even a bit pushy. But in that instant, with Liz's health hanging in the balance, everything else faded away. I was her voice and advocate, and I wouldn't rest until I felt confident she was getting the care she deserved. It felt like a fight, not just for Liz's health but for her comfort and well-being, too.

I started small, doing everyday tasks like brushing her teeth and combing her hair. While doing so, I noticed her hair was tangled and matted from her ordeal. I worried we might have to cut it all off, a heartbreaking prospect. Then, one evening, two angels in the form of nursing aides surprised us.

They spent hours gently untangling the knots and braiding her hair with surprising skill, bringing tears to my eyes. Amidst the harsh reality of the hospital, these medical professionals offered a glimpse of kindness and humanity that I'll never forget.

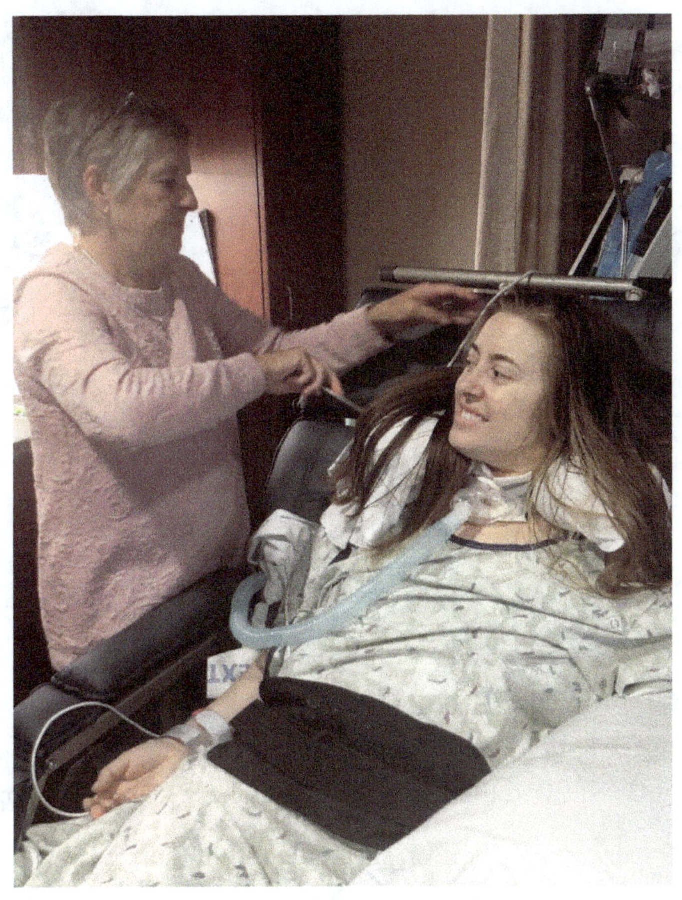

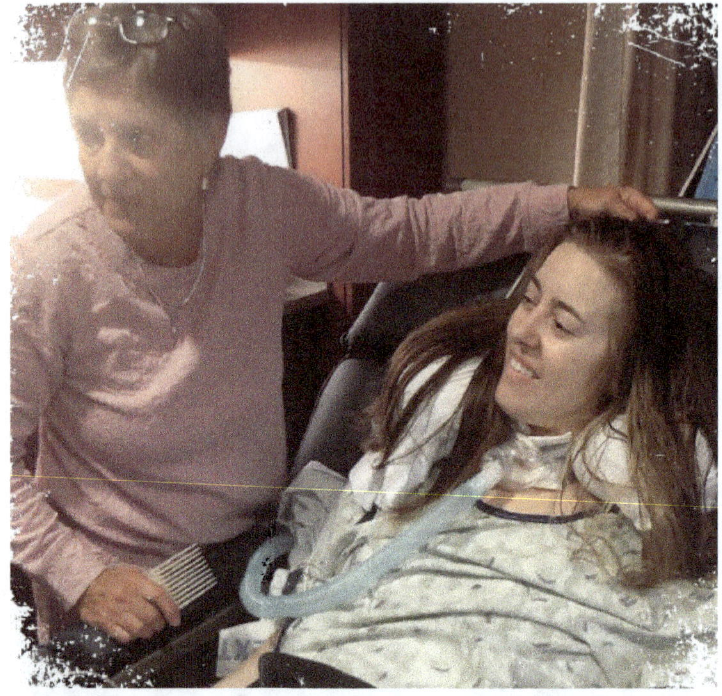

As I cared for Liz, taking over her routine chores, I was struck by a thought. Music had always been a major part of her life, bringing her immense joy and comfort. Perhaps surrounding her with things she loved from before this ordeal would help. So, I brought in my portable speaker, hoping to spur a connection. As the familiar sounds of Little River Band filled the room, I watched her eyes slightly open.

A spark of recognition surfaced within them, and with her head resting on the pillow, she began to mouth the words perfectly. Tears streamed down my face, not out of sadness but pure, unadulterated hope. Despite the tubes and monitors and the paleness in her body, Liz was still there. Her love for music, a constant throughout her life, remained a powerful thread connecting us.

In that magical instant, submerged in the soothing melody, a wave of inevitability overpowered me: Liz was a fighter, and with every ounce of strength I possessed, I knew I would be by her side every step of the way, cheering her on as she fought her way back to health.

Upon witnessing these recoveries, Patrick realized it might be the right time for the kids, Paige and Liam, to see their mom again. The last time they had seen her wasn't a happy memory. It was a frightening image of Liz, unconscious and in pain, on the day of her cardiac arrest. The initial days that followed in the ICU were a blur of machines and monitors, constantly reminding all of us how fragile her life had become.

We instinctively knew that seeing her in that state would only terrify the children, as their young minds would try to piece together the unfamiliar sights and news.

With a heart full of hope yet tinged with nervousness, Patrick made arrangements for a visit on the weekend. It would be a sentimental reunion, but Patrick knew deep down that it was a step forward, a chance for Paige and Liam to reconnect with their mom and the entire family to begin the long healing journey together. The very thought of reuniting as a family brought a lump to Patrick's throat— a fierce sense of protectiveness.

Steadily, the weekend arrived, and with it came a wave of panicky excitement. The joy on Liz's face was undeniable when the kids were finally brought into her room. Tears welled in her eyes as she listened to Paige and Liam chatter excitedly about school and their lives. It was a simple conversation, far from the ordinary, yet filled with the everyday details that had been absent for so long. Right then and there, it felt like everything.

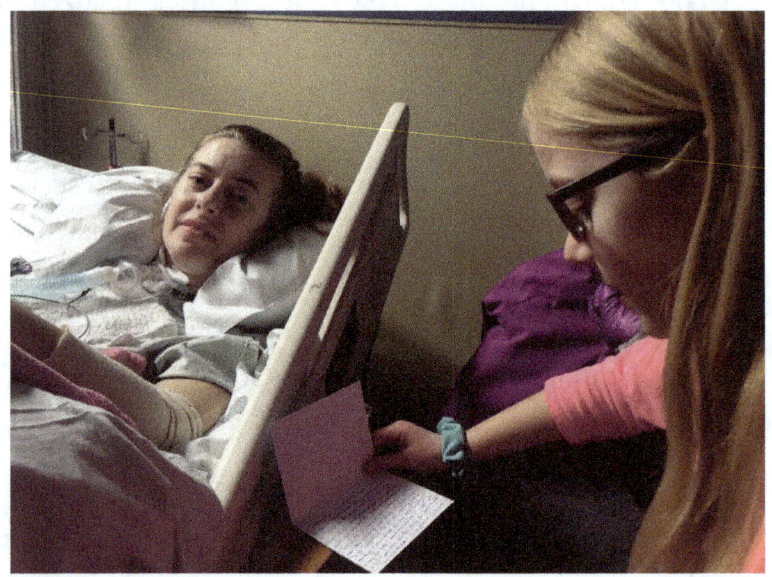

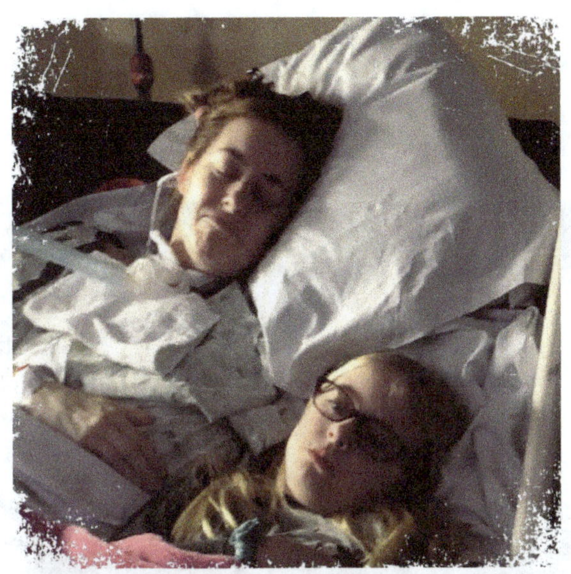

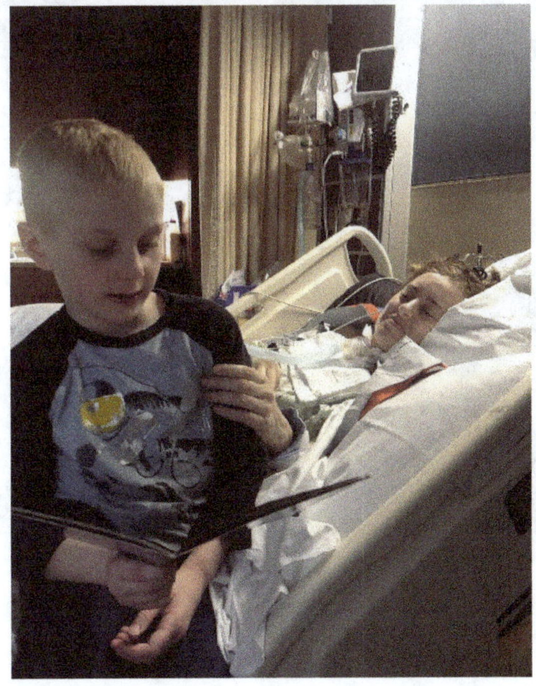

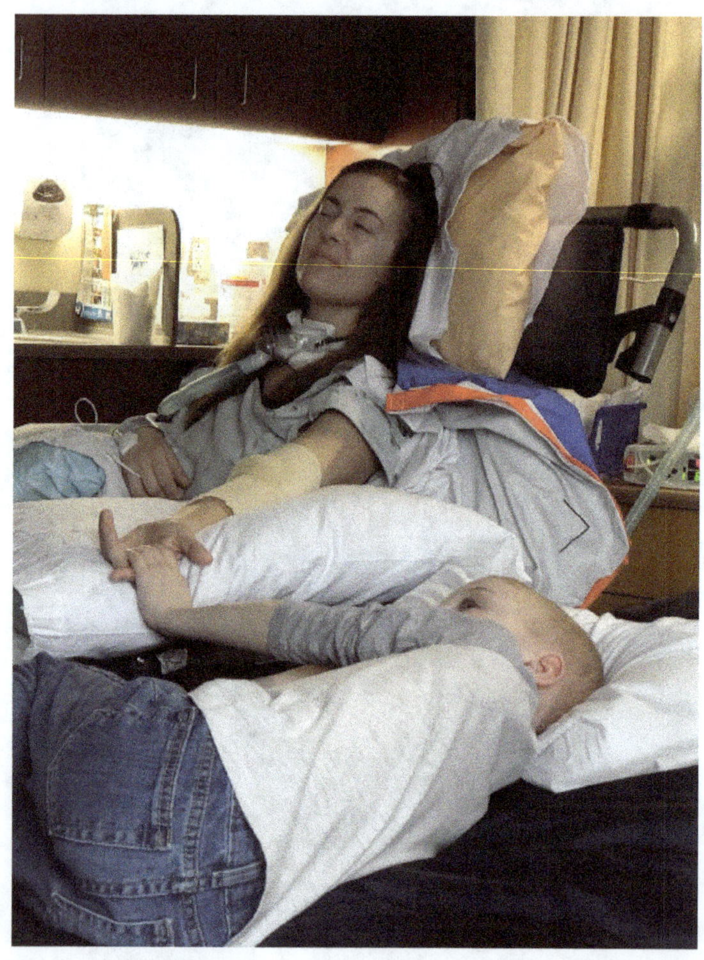

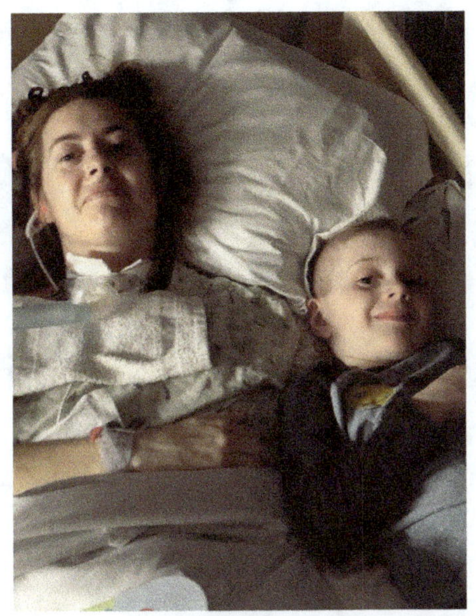

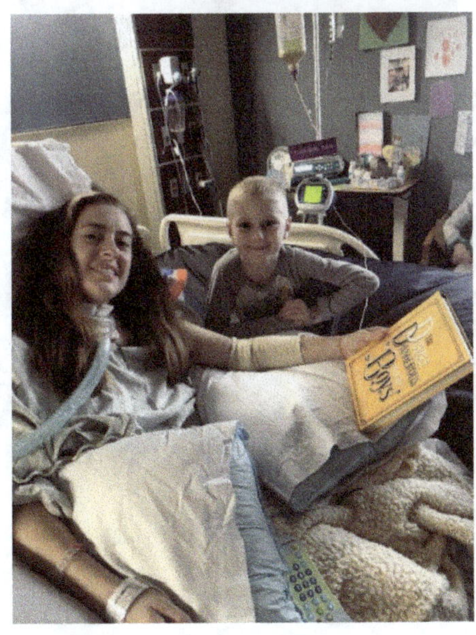

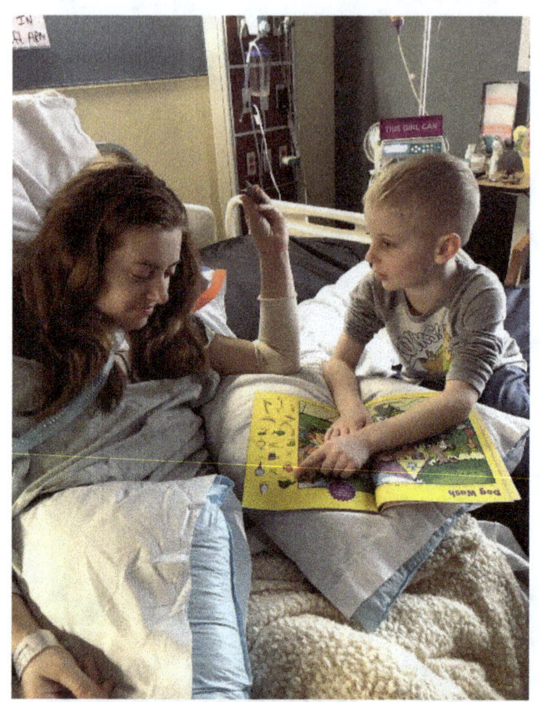

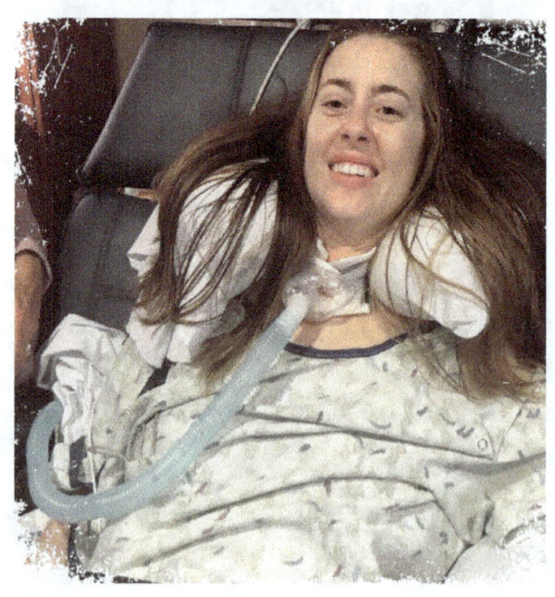

Paige even managed to paint a wobbly but colorful design on Liz's toenails. It was a small act, a touch of normalcy that brought relief coursing through Patrick. They carefully chose bright colors, knowing Liz loved having her nails done. Liz watched them with a soft smile, her eyes showing how much she appreciated the gesture.

Steadily, as days passed, Patrick and I clung to the idea that Liz might be home by Christmas, a vision of family gatherings and shared joy that drove our resolve. It was a goal, a target that kept us focused and hopeful. But then came the news: a four-week stay at Mary Free Bed, followed by a return home, all under the new shadow of COVID restrictions. Only Patrick could visit Liz now, the physical distance layering itself on top of the emotional one. It felt isolating, a constant ache of wanting to be closer, to be there for her in person.

Settling into Mary Free Bed, the reality of the path ahead became clear. Liz wasn't walking yet, and movement on her right side was limited. It was an obstacle, a sobering reminder of the journey she was treading on. Our optimism, however, remained strong. Despite the limitations, there were glimmers of ease. In the mornings, Liz seemed alert and engaged. She mouthed answers to some questions, her voice still weak but her mind sharp. Liz was still weak, her movements limited, but a spark in her eyes refused to fade away.

The shift to rehab was a fragile start, a tentative first step in regaining stability. But we knew we would face it together. We would be there for each other, putting up a united front against whatever challenges lay ahead, rebuilding our lives stronger than ever before.

Chapter 8: A New Beginning

Each day at Mary Free Bed brought encouraging signs of Liz's recovery. Although tiring, the therapy sessions pushed her body forward, and the sight of Patrick during his visits filled her with a sense of joy that warmed our hearts.

As a family, we were immersed in immense exhaustion, determined to ensure Liz received the rest she needed to regain her strength and return home as soon as possible.

Meanwhile, the world around us was reshaped by the ever-present threat of COVID-19. News reports were filled with constant updates about rising death tolls. A sense of unease settled in, a low hum of worry underscoring every aspect of daily life.

Yet, amidst this changing landscape, Liz continued to amaze me. Her world, too, was undergoing a transformation, a journey of healing and determination that unfolded one step, one small victory at a time.

We, as a family, adapted to this dual transformation. Confronted with the prospect of limited visits and the ever-present risk of the virus, we found new ways to stay connected and support Liz. Through it all, Liz's courage and willpower inspired us. Watching her fight to recover daily was a powerful reminder of her strength and resilience. Every little progress in her condition fueled our hope and faith to achieve the normalcy we craved as a family.

While we knew, with profound certainty, that she was on her way to recovery, the mere thought of having her back home with us during that tiresome time sent a jolt of excitement through us. The idea of having a familiar face in an increasingly unfamiliar world filled us with an almost unbearable longing. We couldn't wait for the day she could return, the day our family circle would be whole again. The thought of her laughter resounding through the house again, the warmth of her presence filling the space at dinner tables and family gatherings, were the dreams that ran our optimism.

Liz's therapy sessions were exhausting, a demanding three hours a day divided between physical, speech, and occupational therapy. While fatiguing, they were also a source of immense excitement. Each session brought new challenges, new hurdles to overcome, and with them, the promise of further progress. It was one of those days at the rehab when a monumental achievement was unlocked: Liz managed to sit up in the wheelchair twice! The effort drained her, but a triumphant smile appeared on her lips.

Through the most difficult parts of her treatment, Liz persevered. Confusion sometimes clouded her mind, fragments of memory struggling to piece together recent events. Yet, there were moments of lucidity, flashes of her old self shining through. She would ask questions, her voice weak but her resolve staunch, determined to understand what had happened to her. It was a long road ahead, filled with challenges and obstructions, but Liz was a warrior. Her untiring spirit and grit to reclaim her life inspired us all.

Amid these struggles, a ray of sunshine arrived. Our family received a beautiful gift just a week before Liz's admission to Mary Free Bed. My daughter, Mary, gave birth to a healthy baby girl, Emma. It was a moment of pure joy, a reminder of life's preciousness even amidst hardship.

Becoming a grandma again filled me with a love that rivaled the worry nibbling at my heart.

Showing Liz a picture of Emma brought a wave of emotions that day. Her face lit up with a love that transcended her physical limitations. It was a beautiful moment, reminding us of the connections and familial love that bind us together, even in the face of adversity. And so, between the joy of a new grandchild and the daily victories

of Liz's recovery, my days were filled with a complex mix
of emotions.

The following weekend, after little Emma came into the world, truly tested my capacity to juggle. Mary needed all the support she could get with the baby's arrival. Balancing my time with Liz and helping my daughter and her new baby was a challenge. Thankfully, Elizabeth, with her kind heart, stepped in to help. She offered to take care of Mary's older children, easing the burden and allowing me to focus on my immediate family and Liz's ongoing recovery. It was a busy but heartwarming time filled with family and new beginnings.

Elizabeth's generosity, however, extended far beyond that single day. Even before Emma's arrival, she had shown a quiet thoughtfulness that warmed my heart.

The week before the birth, Elizabeth took Paige on a special outing. They ventured to Target, a girls' afternoon filled with laughter and the thrill of picking out a gift for the unborn Emma. The present, carefully chosen and tucked away in a large bag, was a mark of Elizabeth's anticipation and love for the newest member of our family.

Their adventure didn't end there. After Target, they stopped for lunch at McDonald's, a simple act that spoke volumes about Elizabeth's willingness to connect with Paige and the entire family. They spent the afternoon together, a bond forming between aunt and niece before Elizabeth ensured Paige was safely back home before leaving for another errand. Her final act of that day— making dinner for everyone at home further proved her selflessness.

During our challenges, particularly regarding Liz's condition and the hospital visits, these gestures, big and small, filled me with an overwhelming sense of gratitude. We were a family facing a difficult time, yet each member stepped up, offering support and a shoulder to lean on. It was a powerful reminder of the strength that comes from love and unity.

Here, I am reminded of my sister, Karen, who was an invaluable source of support throughout this ordeal. Her presence was a constant source of comfort, offering a quiet companionship that allowed me to focus on Liz's needs without feeling overwhelmed. She would often sit in the waiting room, allowing me to be fully present with Liz. This selfless act of support exemplified the profound impact that family can have during times of crisis.

We had each other, and that, I knew, was the greatest gift of all.

A sense of hope surfaced as I juggled these new family dynamics with Liz's ongoing recovery. Meanwhile, Liz was making significant progress in her therapy back at the rehab center. Resolute to regain her independence, she pushed herself in each session.

Another triumph brought tears to our eyes. During a therapy session, Liz reached for a pen and, with a newfound focus in her eyes, attempted to sign her name. It wasn't perfect, a bit wobbly perhaps, but the familiar loops and curves bore an undeniable resemblance to her pre-illness handwriting. It was a simple act, yet it felt monumental.

The increased strength in her arms wasn't just about numbers on a chart. It meant Liz could finally spend more time sitting up in her chair, a seemingly simple act that felt like a giant leap forward. It allowed her to see the world from a different perspective, a small victory that brought a sense of accomplishment and a glimmer of normalcy back into her life.

This improvement wasn't just physical. Once labored and halting, her speech also showed signs of progress. The previously garbled words now appeared clearer, and the sentences were fully formed. With each improvement, it felt like the fog that clouded her mind was slowly lifting, revealing flashes of the Liz we all knew and loved—the woman who could converse, share a joke and connect with us all. It was a heartwarming sight, a reminder of the dear person we missed.

One day, a moment of pure joy filled the rehab center. With newfound strength and clarity in her voice, Liz began to recite her cell phone number! Each digit came out clear and distinct, directing towards her progress. It might seem like a simple task, a string of numbers anyone could remember. However, considering Liz's initial progress and her previous brain activity while she was in the ICU, it felt massive to us. It meant she was regaining a piece of her individuality, a way to reconnect with the world beyond the walls of the rehab center.

Another hurdle was cleared a few days later. Liz aced her swallow test, a crucial step in her recovery. This meant the restrictions on her diet were lifted! No longer confined to bland or pureed meals, she could finally explore a wider variety of foods. For weeks, the simple act of eating had been a chore due to the limitations on her. However, now, the prospect of enjoying textures and flavors again brought joy to her eyes. It was a sign of regularity returning, a step closer to regaining control over her life.

Liz's positive spirit continued to shine through in surprising ways. Even the hospital food, which most people found unappetizing, appealed to her. Bland mashed potatoes and lukewarm broth seemed like culinary delights to her recovering taste buds. The staff found it amusing, and this lighthearted revelation made us realize how much we take simple pleasures for granted when we're healthy. Liz's returning appetite was a strong indicator of her overall well-being. These small victories and everyday achievements were like bricks laid one by one, building a foundation of hope for the future.

The future now held the promise of a normal life. Every day brought a new challenge conquered, a new skill relearned, and another piece of the old Liz returning. It was a slow and steady process, but as we faced each day head-on, the path to recovery seemed a little clearer, the light at the end of the tunnel a little brighter.

In a way, I had two parts of Liz with me each day: Paige and Liam. Their laughter boomed through the house, reminding us of the joy and life we all fought to reclaim. With Rachael, a school teacher working from home due to COVID protocols, most days, Paige and Liam would spend their mornings attending classes at her house. This arrangement, while temporary, allowed me some much-needed time to focus on Liz's recovery and manage household duties. By noon, I'd be there to pick them up, their playful energy a welcome distraction from the anxieties gnawing at me.

At the moment, social distancing, a concept dominating the news and everyday life, wasn't a realistic option for our family. We were a unit, bound by love and a fierce grit to navigate this challenging time together. Even though I ached for Liz's physical presence, having Paige and Liam by my side filled a void I hadn't realized existed. Their innocent smiles and constant need for love and attention kept me grounded, summoning up my introspections that life, despite its hardships, continued to offer moments of joy and connection. In the quiet moments, between picking them up from playdates and sharing stories of their day, I found a revived strength that kept me going on most days.

To this day, the children have chosen not to discuss the traumatic event. Liam vividly recalls the day of the incident, describing the frightening moment when he saw his mother unresponsive. On the other hand, Paige has opted to cope with the experience by avoiding the topic altogether. We respect their decision to process the event in their own way and time. Their resilience in the face of such trauma portrayed their strength and adaptability.

On a lighter note, as I talked with Liz on FaceTime daily, I couldn't help but smile at the imaginative stories she shared. One day, she told me she had been incredibly busy, having traveled to Hawaii, California, and Detroit—all in just one day. It was clear that her brain was working overtime, creating a reality where she could escape, even if just for a moment. These conversations, though rooted in confusion, brought a sense of levity to an otherwise heavy situation, reminding me of the mind's incredible capacity to adapt and find solace, even in the most trying times.

As each morning dawned, it brought a sense of purpose that we all desperately gripped. We were closer to reuniting our family, a day closer to a life that felt normal again. Looking back on Liz's journey, it felt like a miracle was unfolding before our eyes. The progress she had made defied the initial prognosis. When she first arrived at rehab, her condition was terrifyingly critical. Yet, here she was, steadily recovering, as a result of her steadfast willpower to recover, along with the incredible care she was receiving from the medical professionals at the hospital.

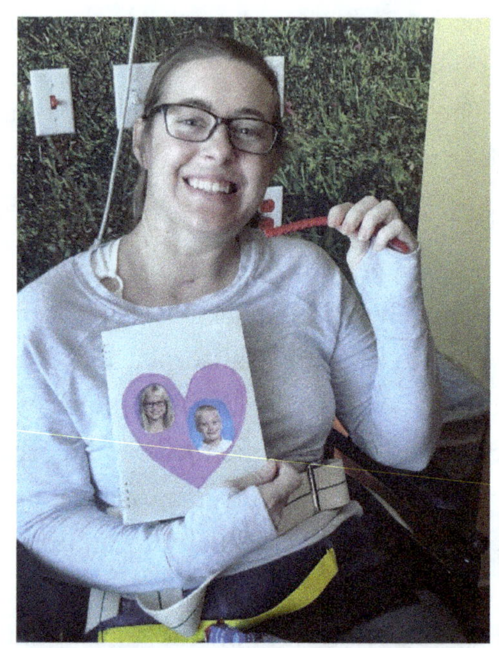

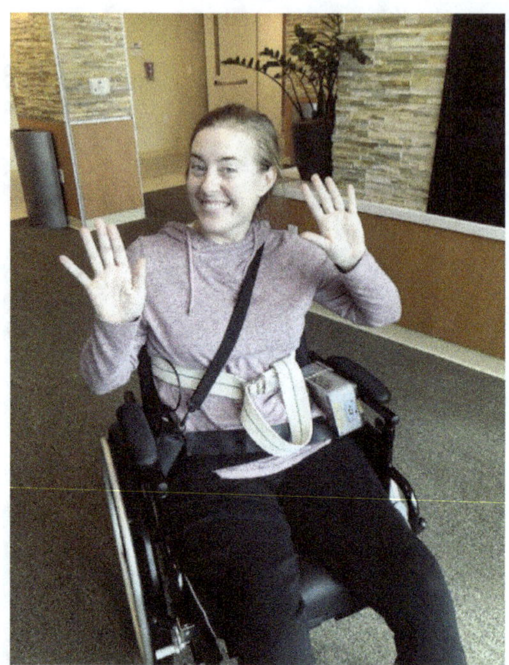

My heart swelled with deep pride for Patrick throughout this ordeal. He stood by Liz's side with untiring strength during her most vulnerable moments. He was the embodiment of a devoted partner, a husband whose love shone through every action. Restricted by hospital regulations, his visits were precious. Yet, during those limited interactions, he made the most of them. He would hold Liz's hand, his contact a silent promise of love and support.

However, his dedication extended far beyond these visits. He was Liz's rock through and through, a constant source of strength as she navigated the challenging path to recovery. Confined to isolation within the rehab center, Liz faced therapy sessions that pushed her physically and mentally.

But she wasn't alone. Patrick was her champion, by her side, offering her immense comfort.

Together, they were a team, a united front facing every obstacle head-on. Their love, a powerful force, burned brightly even in the face of adversity. Thus, Patrick's dedication wasn't just a source of strength for Liz; his presence was a source of incredible love and support that surrounded us all and filled us with a deep sense of gratitude.

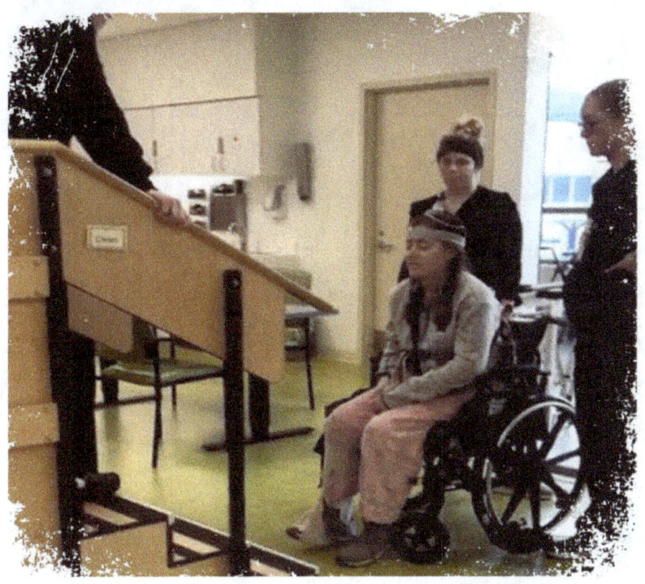

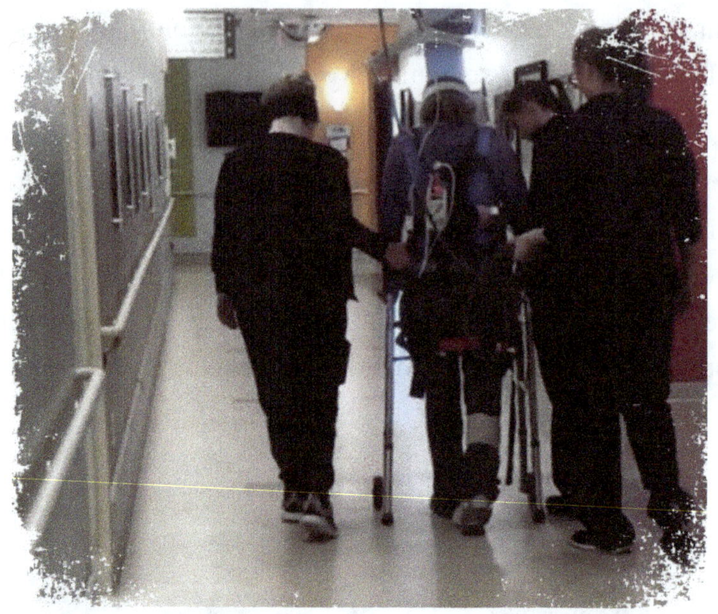

Meanwhile, Liz's therapy sessions were a battlefield of determination. Physical therapy pushed her boundaries, getting her back on her feet and, to everyone's surprise, even climbing stairs! Each conquered step was a triumph, a cheer echoing through the hospital halls. It was a silent promise of a future where she could walk freely again.

The progress extended beyond physical gains. Occupational therapy focused on daily tasks, seemingly mundane things like dressing herself each morning. Yet, it felt like reclaiming a piece of herself back for Liz. Each button fastened and sleeve pulled on was a tiny success - a brick laid on the path back to normality.

During those days at rehab, the afternoons brought a change of pace: a furry friend! A therapy dog visit brightened Liz's day. With its wagging tail and wet nose nudges, the playful pup showered Liz with unconditional love. It would sit patiently by her side, letting her stroke its soft fur, offering a furry shoulder to lean on as she confided in it, or simply enjoying its playful presence in the room. The playful pup's unconditional love brought a smile to her face.

Through each update in her treatment at rehabilitation, we clung to every shred of hope, every scrap of progress. Therapy sessions, doctor's visits, and even the playful visit from the therapy dog were all major sources of support thrown into the storm that was Liz's recovery. We grasped at them all, desperate to find anything that would pull her back to the surface, anything that could guide her out of the chaos and back to the life we all longed for.

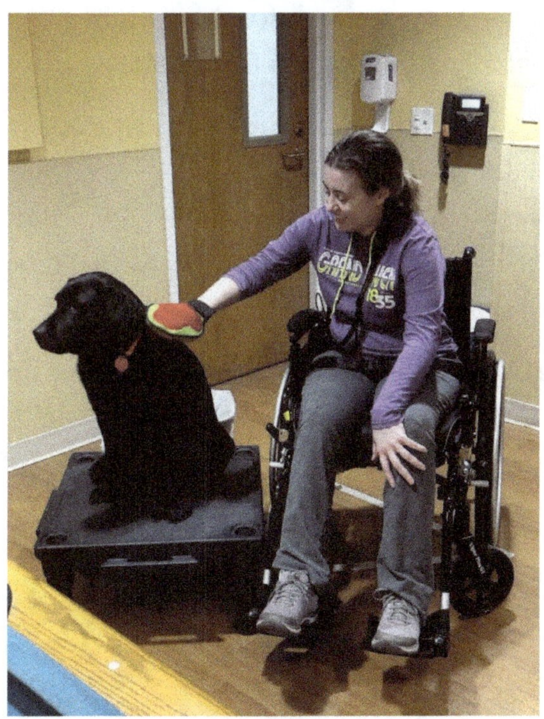

Gradually, March receded, one month that seemed like an eternity, finally paving the way for April. With each passing day, hope bloomed brighter. Liz remained on track for her mid-April homecoming. Her hard work in therapy was evident in her remarkable progress. Every session brought her closer to recovery; even a spark of her signature humor had begun resurfacing. It was a subtle change, a hint of the old Liz peeking through, and it fired our anticipation even more.

The kids, especially, were bursting with excitement. Confined by the hospital's strict COVID-19 protocols, they eagerly awaited the moment they could finally reunite with their mom. Once strangely quiet, the house seemed to vibrate nervously as we prepared for her return. We were all preparing for a new chapter, a fresh start.

There would still be challenges to face, of course, but with Liz back home, surrounded by the love of her family, we were ready to tackle them together. Once uncertain due to medical complications, the future now held the potential of hilarity, shared meals, and the simple joys of normal life.

As the days unfolded, filled with anticipation and nervous excitement, we knew that our family would soon be complete again. Liz would be home, where she belonged.

Chapter 9: A Miracle from God

As Liz approached the final week of her stay at Mary Free Bed Rehabilitation, a new hurdle emerged: the strict enforcement of COVID-19 protocols. Unfortunately, these necessary safety measures meant no visitors were allowed. This sudden isolation would prove to be a significant setback for Liz.

Still struggling with confusion, she was unable to fully grasp the situation. The familiar faces and comforting presence of loved ones, especially Patrick, were sorely missed. A question that weighed heavily on her mind, a question we had heard before but taken on new urgency in her isolated state, was whether she and Patrick were actually married. While delivered with love and unwavering certainty, our reassurances seemed to have limited effect.

It was a heartbreaking week that illustrated the emotional toll this isolation could take. We yearned to be by her side, to offer comfort and a sense of normalcy. But for now, all we could do was wait, hoping that with each passing day, the fog of confusion would lift and the reassurance of our love would finally reach her.

Finally, that long-awaited day arrived. Elizabeth's arrival back home felt no less than a miracle from God. Stepping back into the familiar walls of her house, she was met with a wave of overwhelming emotion. Her children were the first to greet her, rushing into her arms with tearful joy. My embrace, filled with relief and love, followed soon after.

In preparation for her return, we made a few adjustments to the house. Mark, ever resourceful, installed handrails on both sides of the stairs and down the hallway. Thankfully, the stairs were short, making navigation slightly easier. She used a walker for added stability for a while, gradually regaining her confidence with each step.

The children, especially, were a constant source of support at this time. They showered her with love and protectiveness, a heartwarming display of their bond. Their absence during her stay at MFB had weighed heavily on them. I recall one evening, just before her discharge, the silence in the house felt deafening. We were all gathered around the TV, forcing a sense of normalcy in the face of our longing. Liam, usually brimming with energy, snuggled into my lap. Moments later, with her big eyes filled with unspoken sadness, Paige asked if there was room for her too. At that moment, the depth of their yearning for their mother was laid bare, a poignant reminder of the strength of our family unit, which had been put to the test.

Once back home, Liz's progress continued on a steady incline. Each day brought measurable improvements in both confidence and stability. The handrails and walker remained crucial tools, offering security during movement. However, the most significant factor in her recovery was the love and support of her family. We were by her side every step of the way, offering practical assistance whenever needed.

Challenges, of course, were inevitable. New tasks and routines presented hurdles, but we faced them together—a united family tackling each obstacle one step at a time. The children, in particular, impressed us with their adaptability. They quickly embraced the new routine, readily offering help around the house whenever possible. Their understanding of Liz's limitations was evident in their gentle demeanor, and they even offered quiet companionship, simply being there for their mom when she needed them most. Their love and care, expressed in countless ways, became a significant force propelling her recovery forward.

The next step on that journey involved outpatient rehabilitation. We meticulously scheduled and prepared for these visits, with me accompanying Liz to most of them.

These sessions, spread across several days a week and continuing well into August, focused on various aspects of her recovery. Speech therapy helped Liz regain control over her communication skills, while occupational therapy equipped her with the tools to navigate daily tasks. Physical therapy, of course, remained crucial, strengthening her body and improving her mobility.

Moreover, the rehabilitation center conducted extensive mental ability testing. Here, Liz surprised everyone, scoring remarkably high on the evaluations. It was a testament to her strength and resilience, a sign that her mind, like her body, was on the path to healing.

After a few initial sessions, however, I noticed a shift.

Perhaps seeking comfort in a familiar face, Liz often relied on me for answers during her therapy sessions.

Realizing this could hinder her progress, I decided to step back and allow her to tackle these challenges independently. It wasn't easy, but it was a necessary step in empowering her to rediscover her voice and reclaim her autonomy.

Liz's biggest challenge, however, resided in the realm of her memory. The strokes had significantly impacted her ability to form and retain new memories. Simple tasks presented a formidable hurdle, like remembering a conversation from just moments ago. While seemingly intact in some areas, her long-term memory contained large gaps. During her rehabilitation, she experienced moments of confusion regarding her personal relationships. She clearly remembered her family members but could not recall being married to Pat. This period was marked by uncertainty, as she mistakenly believed she was divorced, though she couldn't exactly identify from whom. This situation was particularly challenging given Pat's close relationship with her. Familiar faces and places could trigger no recollection, leaving her feeling disoriented and confused.

The familiar surroundings of her house held no recognition for her. The move from Indianapolis to Spring Lake, a significant life event, seemed to have vanished entirely. She felt like she had been "gone" for years, a disorienting sense of lost time stretching before her like a hazy fog. Everyday details, large and small, presented constant confusion. Picking up a familiar object might elicit no recognition, the once-automatic association severed by the stroke's damage. Even the physical environment of her own home felt alien. Each morning, she would wake up disoriented, almost as if it were the first day she had ever been there. Once a source of comfort and familiarity, the world around her felt like a foreign land she had to navigate anew.

This disorientation was further compounded by significant gaps in her memory, extending beyond the immediate aftermath of the stroke. It became apparent that she had lost access to a substantial portion of her life experiences, primarily three years before the ordeal, including pivotal family events such as my and Mark's wedding in 2017. This realization highlighted the extent of the neurological impact the stroke had on her cognitive abilities.

One can only imagine the immense frustration this must have caused her. Doctors informed us that the brain's healing process could take anywhere from 18 months to three years—a seemingly long and arduous road ahead. Medically, this timeframe reflects the brain's remarkable neuroplasticity capacity and ability to reorganize and form new connections between neurons. Following a stroke, damaged areas of the brain may not be able to recover fully, but the brain can compensate by rerouting functions to healthier parts. This process, however, is gradual and requires consistent stimulation through therapy and daily activities. While three years seemed daunting, it also represented a window of opportunity, a chance for Liz's brain to heal.

Considering the generally assumed aftereffects of a stroke, which often include disruptions in memory function, Liz surprised us all with her remarkable progress! I vividly remember when, one day, my brother Ron approached her cautiously, unsure how she would react.

"Hi Liz, it's Uncle Ron," he said tentatively.

And then, a radiant smile lit up her face. "Uncle Ron, of course, I know you!"

This simple exchange offered reassurance that the connections forged over a lifetime were not lost forever but slowly restored. It meant that with continued therapy and support, Liz might eventually reclaim her physical abilities and the relationships that made her life so meaningful.

There were also other moments of joy and sheer comfort. Liz was finally home, surrounded by the love and support of her family. This environment, filled with cherished faces, offered much-needed well-being and security. It was definitely dissimilar to the isolation and uncertainty she had experienced during her hospitalization.

While my visits with her to attend her PT, OT, and ST sessions comforted me in knowing I was there with her, I soon became exhausted from the emotional toll. Watching her struggle, yet witnessing her determination, was a constant tug-of-war on my heart. Occupational therapy, in particular, presented challenges I simply couldn't replicate at home. Some tasks required specialized equipment or techniques that fell outside my expertise.

However, Liz's progress brought a wave of relief and a renewed sense of optimism. Her right leg, once weak and unstable, was steadily regaining strength. A recent breakthrough saw her completing her physical therapy exercises without the brace, a demonstration of her dedication and the effectiveness of the therapy. The therapists were impressed with the overall improvement in her strength, not just in her leg but throughout her body. Her right hand, previously weaker than her left, now displayed a firmer grip, a crucial step toward regaining her independence. While writing remained a slight hurdle, it was a challenge she was steadily overcoming with each passing day.

Medically, these improvements signified the remarkable regenerative capacity of the nervous system. As Liz performed repetitive exercises, the damaged neural pathways in her brain were being stimulated and rerouted. As mentioned earlier, this process, known as neuroplasticity, allowed her to regain control over her movements and relearn lost skills. It was a slow process indeed, but the visible progress fueled our hope and willpower to see her recovery through to completion.

Of course, there were still moments of vulnerability.

"I feel like such a burden, with all these visits and you taking care of me all the time," Liz confided in me one day.

"But honey, you won't always be like this. You're getting stronger every day. And besides, someday the tables might turn, and I might need you to look after me," I reassured her jokingly.

A weak smile formed on her lips. "That's true, Mummy," she said with a slight chuckle.

It was a trivial moment, but it demonstrated her resilience and her spirit to get better. She could still find humor and a sense of perspective even amidst her struggles. It offered a glimpse of the woman she was before the medical complications: the woman with a quick wit and a positive outlook.

Liz's untiring spirit continued to surprise me in the most unexpected ways. One day, after her outpatient rehab session, we were driving toward Grand Haven when I was stopped for speeding. In her typical light-hearted manner, Liz asked if she should act like something was wrong with her. When the policeman asked her why she was wearing a brace on her leg, she replied, "I had several strokes."

Showing some understanding, the officer gave me a break but still issued a ticket. We continued our drive to the Grand Haven shoreline, and to my delight, everything seemed familiar to her. We would have stopped for lunch, but as you might have guessed, the restaurants were closed due to COVID-19 restrictions.

We were still working on memory and everything, of course. While some things remained frustratingly elusive, other abilities, like her amazing math skills, seemed remarkably intact. Her mind was in overdrive, actively working to rewire itself and forge new connections. This intense mental effort, however, left her understandably exhausted by the end of the day.

But we continued to believe in her. We knew that with time, patience, and continued therapy, she would gradually overcome these challenges.

A few days later, a significant milestone was achieved. It was Memorial Day weekend, and we were celebrating Liz's birthday! Liz turned 39 on May 25, 2020. Just a few months earlier, I had witnessed her struggle to regain her footing, and the thought of celebrating another birthday had seemed unimaginable.

How could we possibly get through this difficult time? I had wondered.

Yet, here we were, surrounded by loved ones, celebrating another year of Liz's life.

The Spring Lakers, our close-knit community, gathered with Mark and me to shower Liz with love and support. Despite lingering fatigue from a recent defibrillator placement, Liz smiled warmly and enjoyed the afternoon festivities. A surprise visit, albeit socially distanced, from Aunt Patty and Uncle Paul, whom Liz hadn't seen in months, brought an extra layer of joy to the occasion. It was a reminder that even during challenges, there were moments of pure happiness and connections to cherish.

These moments fueled our determination as we witnessed Liz's progress firsthand. At therapy, significant strides were being made. The walker, once a constant companion, was finally retired! Her therapists were confident she could manage walks without its assistance, although a supportive brace remained for uneven terrain or longer distances. Liz had set personal goals to address her short-term memory challenges. She actively participated in therapy sessions, diligently working on the tools and techniques designed to help her regain control over this vital cognitive function.

Although there were still setbacks and moments of frustration when memories remained elusive, these were overshadowed by immense joy.

One day, Liz came over for lunch after therapy. A familiar smile lit her face as she walked through the door, which felt like a glimpse into the past. There we were, sitting at the table, chatting and laughing just like we used to. It was a simple moment that filled my heart with a profound sense of normalcy. She had questions about the future of her recovery, and I reassured her with unwavering confidence.

"You've got this, Liz!" the words tumbled out, portraying my immense pride in her strength and determination.

These moments, once a distant dream during the long, harrowing days in the hospital, were now a cherished reality. Each time she walked through the door on her own, that simple "Hi, Mummy!" brought a wave of relief and joy that enveloped me. It was a stark contrast divergence to the agonizing nights spent by her bedside and the constant worry stamped onto my face as I monitored the whirring machines and glowing lights. Now, the sound of her voice, a melody I once feared I might lose, filled the house with a newfound warmth. It was a reminder that love, perseverance, and family support could truly work miracles.

Liz, however, remained humble throughout her recovery. Despite her remarkable progress, she still yearned to fulfill the roles that mattered most to her: as a wife, mother, daughter, sister, aunt, and friend. These connections, intricately intertwined into her life, truly motivated her.

Every day, I thanked God for the gift of Liz's return. Seeing her reclaim her independence, strength, and capacity to love and be loved was a profound blessing. She continued to amaze me with her strength and willpower to rebuild her life. Witnessing her progress, inch by inch, day by day, finally allowed my pain to begin to recede.

It wasn't a sudden vanishing act but a gradual easing, like the tide rolling back after a storm. The fear and uncertainty that had gripped me for so long slowly loosened their hold. Hope and a quiet joy in simply being together again bloomed in their place. We had already survived the toughest ordeal, and the strength we had forged in that crucible would see us through whatever came next.

Chapter 10: Reflections and Realizations

We, Liz's entire family, were overwhelmed with gratitude for the progress she was making. It felt like a miracle unfolding before our eyes. Just a few weeks earlier, we had witnessed her struggle to regain basic motor skills, with fear and uncertainty hanging heavy in the air. Now, here she was, walking on her own, laughing with us, slowly piecing her life back together.

It was a sheer portrayal of her steadfast spirit and the tireless efforts of her therapists. Each milestone, big or small—whether it was a remembered conversation, a completed therapy session, or a simple walk in the park—felt like a victory, a cause for immense celebration. We cherished these moments, savoring the return of the woman we loved so dearly.

However, the journey wasn't without its challenges. The aftereffects of the strokes were still very real for Liz. Her brain, working diligently to rewire itself, often confused her. Everyday tasks and familiar situations became puzzling, like lost pieces in a forgotten puzzle.

There were gaps in her personal history, chunks of memories missing that left her frustrated. In those moments, we patiently helped her navigate the confusion, piecing together fragments of her past.

There were also subtle changes in her personality. Her perception of things and her thinking seemed slightly altered at times. Perhaps it was a consequence of the brain injury, or maybe it was simply a part of her journey toward healing. As her mother, I may have been more attuned to these subtle shifts, but overall, Liz remained remarkably herself.

The challenges, however, extended beyond her recovery. Integrating Liz back into our daily routine required constant adjustments. Thankfully, Patrick shouldered a significant portion of the responsibility, handling many household tasks with untiring support. The children, too, adapted remarkably well. They readily helped their mom with everyday tasks and assisted her as she slowly trod toward regaining her old self.

Yet, even as the children settled into a routine with the evolving dynamics at home, a shadow lingered. Despite the progress, their silence about the stroke was a source of concern. Was it a sign of unspoken fear or perhaps a coping mechanism they had yet to articulate? Only time would tell.

In the meantime, I focused on creating a safe and supportive environment for Liz's recovery. As she diligently attended her cardiac and physical therapy sessions, I made a conscious effort to provide her with opportunities to regain her independence. One such opportunity presented itself during our drives to therapy.

Initially, the thought of letting her back behind the wheel was unnerving. But as her motor skills steadily improved, I made the decision to let her take control. At first, it was a tentative process, a gradual return to a familiar activity. But with each passing session, her confidence grew. Her grip on the steering wheel became steadier, and her maneuvers more precise. Physical therapy, it seemed, had addressed more than just her physical limitations. It had empowered her to reclaim a sense of control over her life.

And there she was, my brave Liz, steering through the city streets with renewed confidence. These moments filled me with immense pride, showcasing the remarkable progress she had made. The impossible, once again, had become possible.

Liz was starting to improve emotionally and mentally. Her once-sharp wit was returning, and her confidence was soaring. Dare anyone challenge her on a math problem! She would swiftly scan the numbers, and then, in a matter of seconds, followed by a quick explanation that was clear and concise, she would present the solution. Moments like these signified the return of her cognitive abilities, a vital piece of the puzzle clicking back into place. It meant that Liz wasn't just recovering physically—she was also reclaiming her intellectual prowess.

Thankfully, this positive trend continued. Three months post-stroke, Liz underwent a neuropsychological evaluation—a comprehensive assessment aimed to detect any lingering cognitive issues, such as psychosis or hallucinations. The medical professionals were pleased to report that Liz showed no signs of these conditions! It was a significant milestone, depicting the remarkable healing power of the brain.

In Liz's case, the damaged neural pathways were slowly being rerouted, with new connections forming to compensate for the ones lost. This ongoing process, while extraordinary, wasn't instantaneous. It required dedicated therapy and determination, both of which Liz possessed in abundance. The absence of any signs of psychosis or hallucinations during her evaluation was a positive indicator that this neuroplasticity was functioning effectively.

Encouragingly, Liz's recollection of events supported this notion. During the clinical assessment, she displayed a clear memory of the strokes themselves, even pinpointing their location in her brain. The details of her extended hospitalization, the therapy sessions at Generation Care, and the ongoing support she received from speech pathology, occupational therapy, and physical therapy at Mary Free Bed—all of it remained remarkably intact.

This wasn't just passive recall—Liz actively participated in her recovery. She had developed coping mechanisms, like keeping a journal and regularly recounting her history, to strengthen these neural pathways and solidify her memories. This displayed her proactive approach and her resolve to reclaim her life.

Moreover, Liz mentioned that she had recently begun playing the piano again. This seemingly simple activity was, in fact, a powerful tool for cognitive rehabilitation. Playing music engages multiple areas of the brain simultaneously. The frontal lobes, responsible for planning and sequencing, work overtime to coordinate the complex movements required. Motor skills—both gross, large muscle movements and fine, precise finger movements—were challenged as she navigated the keys. Even her auditory processing skills came into play as she interpreted and responded to the sounds she created.

Playing the piano provided a multi-faceted workout for her brain, stimulating various neural pathways and promoting their growth. Liz's resourcefulness and willingness to explore new avenues for healing were driving her progress, and she was determined to reclaim her life.

Her willpower was evident in the results of her clinical examination as well. The administered IQ test revealed outstanding scores, placing Liz in the high average range of intellectual functioning (113). Medically speaking, IQ scores are a standardized measure of cognitive abilities. An IQ of 113 falls within the 81st percentile, meaning Liz scored higher than 81% of the population in her age group on this particular test. This score encompasses two main areas: verbal comprehension and performance IQ.

Liz's verbal IQ score, also in the "high average" range (87th percentile), indicated strong communication skills and a well-developed knowledge base. This suggested that her ability to understand and use spoken and written language had recovered unusually well. While falling within the "average" range (68th percentile), the performance IQ score still represented a significant achievement. This test section assesses non-verbal reasoning and problem-solving skills, often involving visual-spatial tasks. While perhaps not quite as strong as her verbal abilities, this score indicated that Liz's overall cognitive function was returning to normal.

The clinician was particularly pleased to see her performance in social cognition and everyday functioning. Liz's scores in these sections demonstrated a strong ability to understand social situations, cultural norms, and practical aspects of daily life. This meant that she could think clearly and apply that thinking to real-world scenarios, a crucial skill for independent living.

The evaluation also revealed exceptional results in arithmetic and digit span tasks. In simpler terms, these tests assessed her ability to perform calculations and retain information in her short-term memory. Strong performance in these areas indicated that Liz's mental processing speed and concentration had improved significantly. She could grasp complex concepts, hold that information in her mind, and manipulate it effectively. This pointed toward a return to her pre-stroke level of focus and attention to detail, skills that would be invaluable if she ever decided to return to the workforce.

The clinician, impressed with her overall progress, even suggested the possibility of future employment. It was a suggestion filled with hope, a future where Liz could live independently and resume a fulfilling career. The path to recovery might still have some challenges, but with each breakthrough achieved, the horizon grew brighter. Liz's fortitude, coupled with the noteworthy capabilities of the brain, was proving a powerful combination. She was getting better and stronger, one accomplishment at a time.

However, there was an unexpected silver lining to Liz's diagnosis. Cardiac non-compaction of the left ventricle, the underlying cause of her cardiac arrests, is a condition that can sometimes run in families. Thankfully, because of Liz's experience, her sisters, Mary and Emily, are now undergoing preventative treatment. As a result of her diagnosis, all my grandchildren have also undergone heart ultrasounds as a precaution.

Medically speaking, early detection of this condition is crucial. Early intervention, often involving medication to manage heart rhythm and function, can significantly reduce the risk of future complications, such as stroke or heart failure. By identifying this condition early, our family was taking proactive steps to safeguard their health.

It was a reminder that while Liz's journey had been challenging, it had also prompted her loved ones to prioritize their well-being. As Liz continued her remarkable recovery, knowing that her family was taking steps to protect themselves brought her a sense of comfort.

Yet, the journey back to normalcy wasn't without its emotional hurdles. While we all strived to re-establish routines and integrate preventative measures into our lives, there were still lingering triggers. For me, the wail of sirens remained a source of unexpected anxiety. Even though I wasn't present when the ambulance rushed Liz to the hospital, the sounds still evoke a flood of emotions for me.

It was a sharp reminder of that terrifying day, a visceral echo of the fear and uncertainty we had all endured.

Healing, I realized, wasn't just about physical recovery; it was also an emotional journey, one that would take time and patience. This experience, as harrowing as it was, also served as a powerful catalyst for personal growth. It forced me to confront some long-held beliefs, particularly those surrounding faith.

I understood that faith wasn't a passive force to be called upon only in times of crisis. It was a cornerstone, a foundation that needed constant nurturing and attention. Like a garden that thrives with regular care, faith also requires cultivation. There have been moments in my life where I struggled with my faith, questioning its role and doubting its power. Liz's cardiac arrest, a life-altering event, could have entirely shattered my belief. Yet, somehow, amidst the fear and uncertainty, only faith remained. Perhaps it was the support of loved ones, the dedication of medical professionals, or simply the remarkable resilience of the human spirit.

Whatever the source, that belief grew stronger, transforming into a source of relief and strength. It didn't erase the pain, nor did it offer easy answers. But it provided a sense of hope, a belief that even in the darkest times, there was light to be found. This experience, though nearly shattering, had ultimately made me stronger. It forced me to confront my vulnerabilities, re-examine my core beliefs, and ultimately, emerge with a deeper appreciation for the power of faith—not just in times of need but as a guiding light throughout life's journey.

In the face of such adversity, another powerful force emerged: the untiring support of our friends. True friendships, I came to realize, were a treasure to be cherished. These weren't fleeting acquaintances or fair-weather companions; these were the ones who stood by us through thick and thin. Their kindness came in many forms: words of encouragement whispered in quiet moments, visits filled with hope, and a comforting presence that eased the burden we carried.

Liz's medical complications served as an unexpected test of the strength of our social circle. Some friends, like phantoms, drifted away, their support evaporating as quickly as it had appeared.

While painful, this ultimately proved to be a gift. It allowed us to shed unnecessary connections, prune our social circle, and focus on those who truly mattered. In their place, genuine friendships blossomed. The bonds with these friends grew stronger, forged in the crucible of shared hardship. This experience proved that true friendship was a precious commodity, a source of support and love that profoundly enriched our lives.

But perhaps the most profound display of support and genuity came from even closer to home. Speaking of sincere connections, my husband Mark truly deserves the highest praise. Throughout Liz's journey, his dedication and strength were a constant source of consolation for me. He prioritized my well-being, even as my world felt like it was crumbling, putting my needs before his own in a selfless act of love. His care wasn't just helpful but a sheer representation of the power of a good marriage, a partnership that can endure any tribulation together.

Mark's presence and love were the wind beneath my wings. He didn't erase the challenges, but he made them bearable. In the face of adversity, our bond grew even stronger, a beautiful reminder of the profound strength that can be found in a loving partnership. I am incredibly lucky to have him by my side.

In the face of difficulty, our familial bond tightened. Perhaps unconventional in some eyes, we take immense pride in the unit we've built. We are a network of support, a shoulder to cry on in moments of despair, and a source of shared laughter in times of joy. We celebrate each other's triumphs, both big and small, finding strength in our collective experiences. These harrowing experiences and days spent closely together checking up on Liz and her progress ultimately brought us closer, reminding us of the comfort that comes from compassion and the assistance of kinship.

As we move forward, we do so with a transformed appreciation for the power of family, a bond that has persevered through hardship and emerged stronger than ever before.

Chapter 11: Messages of Gratitude and Hope

It is often said that when a family member faces a significant health crisis, the impact reverberates through the entire family. It's not just the individual battling illness who requires support; caregivers and loved ones are also deeply affected. The emotional toll of witnessing a loved one's struggle can be overwhelming, often leading to feelings of helplessness, anxiety, and fear.

The dynamics within the family can shift dramatically as members adjust to new roles and responsibilities. It's crucial to recognize that caring for someone with a serious illness is a marathon, not a sprint. The emotional and physical demands can be exhausting, and caregivers must prioritize their well-being to avoid burnout. Seeking support through therapy, support groups, or open communication with loved ones can provide the necessary tools to cope with the challenges and maintain resilience.

While the focus is naturally on the patient's recovery, it's equally important to acknowledge the experiences of those supporting them. By prioritizing self-care and seeking support, family members can better equip themselves to provide the care and encouragement their loved one needs. In doing so, they strengthen their fortitude and contribute to a more supportive and nurturing environment for the entire family.

As Liz continued her remarkable recovery through therapy at Generation Care, a newfound appreciation for the complexities of caregiving emerged. It wasn't just about physical needs—the psychological toll was equally demanding. The steadfast support of family and friends, including Patrick's family, was instrumental in helping us navigate this challenging path. Yet, I recognized the importance of addressing my emotional well-being to be an effective caregiver. I realized that seeking professional help was essential—A space where I could talk openly about my fears, hopes, and everything in between. It was a place where I could find strategies to cope with stress and anxiety, learn how to support Liz effectively and understand my emotional journey.

The weight of worry and uncertainty, walking through the hospital corridors, had taken a toll on my mental health, and I needed guidance to steer through this unfamiliar territory. It was a difficult decision, but I knew it would ultimately benefit both Liz and me.

I was certain that by prioritizing my well-being, I would be better equipped to support her as she trod toward healing.

And so, I embarked on a parallel journey of self-discovery alongside Liz. I sought professional counseling from the same place, separately, to better understand my emotions, to process the complexities of the situation, and to develop coping mechanisms. During these sessions, a surprising realization emerged: the power of writing as a therapeutic outlet. Through the written word, I could explore my thoughts and feelings, giving voice to the overwhelming emotions. I could chronicle Liz's journey, capturing the highs and lows, the moments of despair, and the glimmers of hope.

In doing so, I found a way to process my experiences, make sense of the chaos, and find consolation in the act of expression. Writing became an unexpected source of strength, a way to navigate the complexities of my emotions. Putting pen to paper or fingers to keyboard allowed me to explore the depths of my feelings, to give voice to the fears and anxieties that often felt overwhelming.

Without a doubt, writing is a powerful tool for emotional processing. It offers a safe space to explore thoughts and feelings, make sense of experiences, and find meaning amid confusion. Through the written word, we can gain perspective, identify patterns, and develop coping mechanisms. It's a way to connect with our inner selves, understand our reactions, and find relief in self-expression. By giving voice to our experiences, we can heal, grow, and emerge from difficult times with renewed strength and purpose.

The act of writing can be therapeutic in several ways. It allows us to externalize our internal experiences, creating a physical representation of our emotions. This externalization can offer a sense of distance, allowing us to examine our thoughts and feelings more objectively. Journaling, for instance, can be a structured approach to this process, providing a consistent outlet for emotional expression. By regularly recording thoughts and feelings, individuals can track their emotional progress over time, identifying patterns and triggers and gaining a deeper understanding of their emotional landscape.

Moreover, writing can serve as a cathartic release, allowing us to process intense emotions and reduce stress. When we put our feelings into words, we can experience a sense of relief and release, as if lifting a weight from our shoulders. This emotional catharsis can be particularly beneficial in times of crisis or trauma, providing a healthy outlet for pent-up emotions. We can develop greater self-awareness, resilience, and emotional intelligence by engaging in writing. It can be a source of comfort, strength, and inspiration, helping us to explore life's challenges with greater clarity and purpose.

As it happened, this new understanding of self-expression extended beyond my own experiences. I began to see how this tool could benefit my entire family.

Interestingly, remembering and writing down our experiences wasn't just a solitary pursuit. It became a shared journey for all of us, bringing us closer as one unit. My immediate family members started to share their thoughts and emotions through written messages, emails, and even handwritten letters. Inspired by this shared experience, my sister, Karen, decided to document her perspective on the journey, capturing the complexities of our emotions and the strength we discovered within ourselves.

Kathy,

As I think about Liz and her journey between life and death at such a young age, I am amazed at how she is now a wife and mother again and is able to function. As I was able to observe her husband's support and optimism and all her family around her, it was heartbreaking to see the pain and grief while Liz was on life support and an elderly neurologist who gave her family no hope. We only imagined a young girl on life support for many years and the hard decisions to be made.

Fortunately, we knew a neurologist from Beaumont Hospital in Detroit who was a niece. The family invited her for a "second opinion," and she gave great hope after detecting brain activity. I will never forget Kathy coming out of that conference room and giving a "thumbs up." as an expression of hope for the first time. I know the real help came in prayer. Liz has 30 cousins on her mom's side, who were praying for a miracle, along with relatives and many, many friends. Liz started to improve bit by bit and eventually was able to be moved to Mary Free Bed for "acute, intensive rehab." God gave Liz a second chance, and she is with us today. A true miracle that has changed many lives forever in believing in prayer.

Karen Rossi.

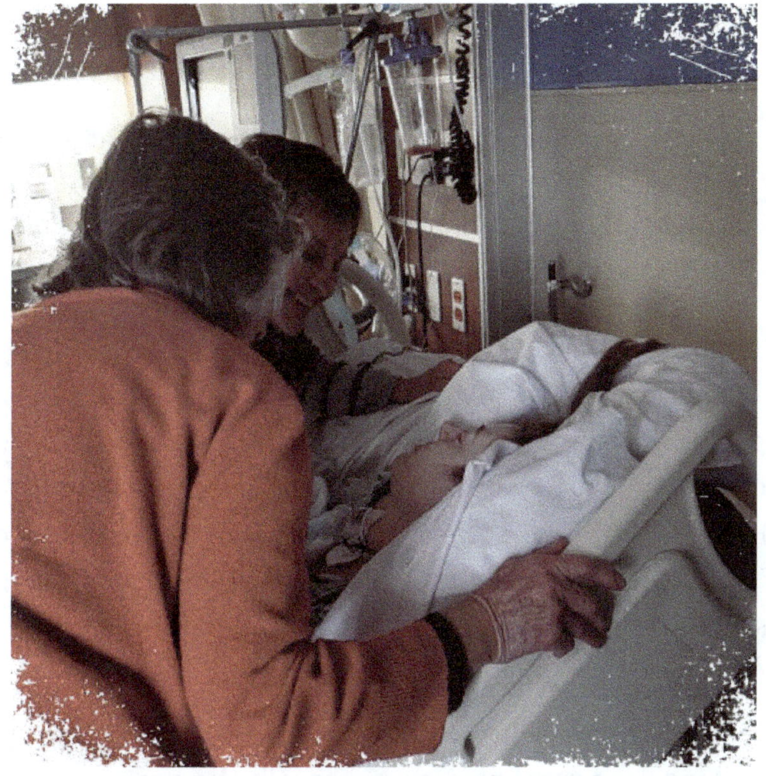

Rick, Karen's husband, also expressed his solidarity in a heartfelt handwritten letter. His words of encouragement and understanding provided an additional layer of comfort during this challenging time.

Hi Kathy & Mark,

Hope this note finds you resting and getting your strength back. The fear and anxiety take their toll. You both have done a wonderful job with Liz, Patrick, their needs, Mary, and the rest of your family.

We all continue to pray with the rest of the family for miracles. Liz has shown determination and fight. With the help of doctors, nurses, and speech specialists, she may one day prove that prayers and family make all the difference.

Patrick has been a rock through all of this. Wonderful for the kids. But, most of all, it's your leadership, confidence, and determination that have made a difference. You are both amazing. God loves you, and so do we. Keep it up!

Rick and Karen.

This unexpected outpouring of vulnerability created a powerful bond among us, deepening our connection and understanding. By sharing our stories, we created a shared narrative. It was a way of acknowledging our shared experiences, validating each other's emotions, and offering support without judgment.

This collective act of storytelling became a source of courage, reminding us that we were not alone in this journey. As I indulged in the process, it gradually dawned on me that by recording and preserving stories, memories, and milestones, families can develop a deeper understanding of their shared history, experiences, and heritage.

This practice can foster a sense of connection and belonging as members explore their individual roles within the family dynamic. Additionally, documenting experiences can be therapeutic, allowing family members to process emotions, gain perspective, and find meaning in shared challenges and triumphs. This collective storytelling process can create a lasting legacy for future generations, preserving family traditions and values for years to come.

Inspired by storytelling's positive impact on our family, I decided to channel my experiences into a tangible form. I wrote a letter to Liz, a heartfelt expression of love, admiration, and support. It was a way to capture the essence of our shared journey, celebrate her willpower, and offer words of encouragement for the path ahead. This letter served as a reminder of our unyielding bond and the strength we found in each other during those challenging times.

Dear Liz,

I see that your faith has grown by leaps and bounds since you have had this near-death experience. Although you don't remember now, you said that you saw Grandma (my mom) in the light, and she told you that you did not belong in heaven yet. You still had things to do on earth.

I see you still struggle with your memory issues, but the light has returned to your eyes. Your gait is still affected by your strokes but seems to improve with all the physical therapy you have put in and your constant daily regimen of self-therapy. So incredibly proud of you.

I have to say you are different. Your personality has changed. Not in a bad way but just different. You have become hyper-focused, which is not a bad thing unless you are driving with me; then, you are the worst backseat driver. Lovingly said.

I want so much for you to develop new friendships, as you were not in Spring Lake long enough for that to happen, and then you became ill. Not sure starting new relationships will be easy for you and maybe it does not even concern you. This could be my issue, not yours. You took a tremendous assault on your brain, and your recovery has been amazing. You are truly one of God's miracles.

I need to finish this true story. It's been hard, and I tried to avoid finishing by doing other things. It makes me so sad to go back there and see you. I wake up sometimes seeing you in that bed in the ICU, and it still makes me cry. The grief was overwhelming. I am so glad you don't remember those horrible days in the hospital. That pain still lies within me when you can't remember everyday things, and I admittedly get tired of you saying, and I am sure you do too, "I can't remember, I have no idea, I don't think so."

I pray every day that you will get some of your memories back, not all of your memories. Yet I am so thankful to God every day that you are right here, being a mom, wife, daughter, sister, and aunt. I am finding closure, a sense of peace. Nothing but blue skies from here on for you. That is my prayer.

I am so extremely grateful and thankful for the love Patrick has for you. He has shown amazing strength through all of this and had to juggle many hats while you were recovering. He told me that you were his life. He loves you so much.

I look forward to seeing you watch Paige and Liam graduate from high school and college, get married, and have children of their own.

Your mother,

Kathy

As I poured my heart out onto the page, expressing my admiration for Liz's strength, I was reminded of the countless individuals who had contributed to her journey. Their support had been a ray of hope during the darkest hours. In particular, the staff at the LTAC unit had provided exceptional care, creating a nurturing environment that fostered Liz's recovery. It was time to express my gratitude and acknowledge their invaluable contributions during a challenging time.

To the Entire Staff of the LTAC Unit of Select Care Hospital,

I apologize for not writing this sooner, but we can't thank you enough for all the wonderful care you gave my daughter, Elizabeth (Liz) Stocker, during her recent stay at the LTAC Unit. Please excuse my typing this, but I was afraid you would be unable to read my writing.

Everyone—doctors, nurses, nursing techs, and the wonderful people who maintain the facilities—has our deepest gratitude and thanks. You all made it easier for us in such a difficult situation and gave us hope when we had very little. We are so excited that Liz is gaining strength as she works hard at MFB in Grand Rapids. She is mastering steps and walking with a walker, and her speech is great. She is on a full diet now and is loving that! We are so thankful that Patrick can continue to see her, and we think she may be home in about three weeks. This is such a strange and difficult time for all of us, but the integrity of all of you during this time makes us realize there is so much kindness and expertise among us.

We want to give you something that you will all enjoy for your unit, but as of now, we cannot do that. If you have any suggestions, that would be wonderful. Even a food gift card would be fine, too. My email is agatha.korte@gmail.com, and though you may feel strange about suggesting anything, I would certainly appreciate it.

Many thanks to all of you, and we pray that you all stay healthy.

Kathy Bailey and Mark Pursley and Families

Patrick Stocker and Family

Emily Quiney and Family

Chris Bailey and Family

Mary Blaicher and Family

Gary Bailey

As I expressed her heartfelt words to Liz and the hospital staff, the experience resonated deeply. It was a poignant reminder that even in the darkest times, when challenges seem insurmountable, God sends an underlying current of hope and perseverance. It is during these trials that we often discover hidden strengths and a capacity for love and compassion that we never knew existed.

In the face of adversity, it becomes evident that life is not merely about overcoming obstacles but about finding meaning and purpose within the struggle. In these moments, we are presented with opportunities to express gratitude, embrace our vulnerabilities, and connect with others on a profound level. Through acts of kindness and compassion, we create a ripple effect of positivity that extends far beyond ourselves.

Chapter 12: Looking to the Future

Both progress and setbacks often mark the journey toward healing. While Liz demonstrated remarkable resilience and achieved significant milestones in her recovery, it was essential to maintain realistic expectations. Persuading ourselves that she would make a full recovery would not only have been unrealistic but could have also created unnecessary pressure and disappointment. It was crucial to acknowledge the lasting impact of the stroke while celebrating her triumphs.

As Liz continued her recovery journey, it soon became evident that certain challenges persisted even after years. Initially, this cognitive impairment impacted her daily life, making it challenging to complete tasks that required sequential processing or the ability to retain information for extended periods. Additionally, the stroke's physical effects were evident in the weakness and reduced mobility of her right leg, particularly after a tiresome day. Despite these challenges, Liz has set her own goals, which include walking the dog daily, spending time on the treadmill, and managing her household chores. Remarkably, she accomplishes all of this without the need for any assistive devices.

Even years after this event, cognitive deficits, particularly concerning memory, continued to pose challenges. To this day, Liz retains no recollection of her eight-week hospitalization period or the house she returned to from the hospital. Her memory remains a void, encompassing her time in the ICU, the step-down unit, and the majority of her rehabilitation at Mary Free Bed. These memory gaps were likely due to the brain's natural reorganization and prioritizing information after an injury. In some ways, it was a relief that Liz retained no recollection of those challenging weeks. The absence of these traumatic memories shielded her from the emotional turmoil associated with those experiences. It allowed her to focus on the present and her ongoing recovery without the added burden of reliving past suffering.

While Liz continued exploring the challenges posed by her stroke, she developed a deep appreciation for the intricacies of the human mind. Now contemplating on her progress and comparing her former self with the present, she claims that while these health developments have taken a significant toll on her physical and mental self, her personality has not changed a bit.

Light-heartedly, she mentioned that she is still the same boring person she always was, acknowledging her increasing tendency towards short-temperedness with a playful chuckle. This self-deprecating humor reflected her willpower to evaluate certain aspects of her personality and her ability to find a comical aspect even when narrating challenging situations.

A coping mechanism like this, often employed as a defense mechanism, allowed her to maintain a sense of normalcy amidst the complexities of her recovery. However, a subtle shift in emotional regulation became apparent beneath this lighthearted exterior.

While Liz exhibited increased emotional reactivity, attributing it to a heightened short temper, it was likely indicative of a broader emotional adjustment. The brain's capacity to regulate emotions is complicated and can be influenced by various factors, including neurological changes. Experiencing a significant health crisis can disrupt these regulatory processes, leading to amplified emotional responses. It is plausible that Liz was experiencing a sharp sensitivity to emotional stimuli, resulting in amplified emotional reactions, which she perceived as an increasingly short temper.

Despite these limitations and vulnerabilities in her progress, Liz, to this day, portrays remarkable courage in living a fulfilling life. While fatigue and physical discomfort occasionally present obstacles, her spirit remains strong. Liz's tireless spirit propels her forward, even on days when the medical implications of this ordeal seem to bring her down. What mattered most for us, as her family, was that she had survived, that she was alive and thriving, albeit with new challenges.

Liz's resolve to rebuild her life inspired those around her. Her medical journey served as a powerful reminder that it is possible to find meaning, purpose, and happiness even in the face of significant hardship. By focusing on progress rather than perfection, she depicted an extraordinary ability to overcome obstacles and live a fulfilling life.

Witnessing her steadfastness in supporting and sustaining herself, our focus shifted toward supporting Liz in reaching her full potential within the limitations imposed by her condition. By embracing a mindset of progress rather than perfection, we empowered her to live a fulfilling life while managing the challenges ahead.

Recognizing that complete recovery might not be attainable, we have shifted our focus to enhancing her quality of life. This involved creating a supportive network, providing practical assistance, and celebrating her milestones, no matter how small. By emphasizing personal growth and resilience, we continue to help Liz build a fulfilling life transcending her physical limitations. This holistic approach encompasses her physical well-being and emotional, social, and psychological needs.

Speaking of these pivotal needs, our role as caregivers has gradually evolved from solely providing physical care to becoming partners in her journey of rediscovery. We have learned to adapt to her changing needs, offering flexibility and understanding while maintaining realistic expectations. By fostering a sense of hope and optimism, we encourage Liz to explore new possibilities and pursue her interests, ultimately leading to a richer and more fulfilling life.

As we evaluated and weighed the complexities of Liz's ongoing recovery, our shared faith provided a source of comfort and strength. It offered a framework for understanding our challenges and a sense of purpose during ambiguity. Through prayer and meditation, we found consolation and renewed our commitment to living each day with gratitude and hope.

While medical advancements and professional care played a vital role in Liz's progress, our faith provided the underlying support system. It allowed us to find meaning in our experiences, appreciate the small victories, and maintain a positive outlook, even when we could not configure the true extent of Liz's recovery. Since then, this spiritual foundation has become integral to our lives, guiding us toward a deeper understanding of ourselves and our place in the world.

Reflecting upon the past several years while committing them to writing, I recognize the importance of maintaining a strong faith. When you face difficult times, holding on to hope and trusting in the power of prayer can guide you. Prayer can provide strength and comfort, helping you to stay resilient. In Liz's journey, it was a constant source of support. It uplifted our spirits and gave us the courage to keep going, even when things seemed impossible at one point.

I have begun to wholeheartedly believe that faith is not merely a belief system but a tangible force that can uplift and sustain us during life's trials. It offers purpose, perspective, and inner peace. It provides the strength to endure hardships and the clarity to see beyond immediate difficulties. And so, by sharing my daughter's journey, I hope to inspire others to embrace the power of faith and conviction as a source of well-being and strength. I want others to see how trust in

God can transform lives, providing courage when the world is determined to bring them down.

Another key lesson I have learned is the importance of advocacy and informed decision-making when facing a critical medical situation. Understanding the complexities of a patient's condition is crucial for making informed choices and advocating for their best interests. This requires a comprehensive understanding of the patient's medical history, current condition, and potential treatment options. It also involves asking critical questions, seeking multiple opinions, and actively participating in decision-making.

Imagine being confronted with a life-or-death decision, such as a recommendation to withdraw life support from a 38-year-old patient with detectable brain activity. I still wonder and brim with pure rage at what would have happened if we hadn't explored other options at that moment. This event highlighted the importance of advocating for the patient's best interests and seeking alternative perspectives.

I believe that by questioning medical recommendations and exploring different treatment options, families can make informed decisions that align with their values and beliefs. The notion of facing such a critical decision can be emotionally overwhelming, but it is essential to maintain a strong and assertive stance.

Subsequently, I learned that by staying informed and actively participating in the decision-making process, we can empower ourselves and our loved ones to navigate healthcare challenges more confidently. Effective patient advocacy involves more than just understanding medical terminology and treatment options.

It requires a comprehensive approach that considers the patient's overall well-being, including their physical, emotional, and psychological needs. By actively participating in the healthcare process and communicating openly with medical professionals, patients, and their families, we can ensure their voices are heard and their concerns are addressed. This collaborative approach fosters trust and empowers individuals to take ownership of their health journey.

Moreover, advocacy plays a crucial role in understanding the complexities of the healthcare system. Contemplating insurance policies, treatment options, and available resources can be overwhelming, but by becoming informed and assertive, patients and their families can advocate for access to necessary care, challenge unreasonable decisions, and ultimately improve health outcomes.

This caregiving journey has been a thoughtful learning experience, teaching us the importance of advocacy and perseverance. Even as Liz progresses and gains independence, our commitment to supporting her remains steadfast. We have learned to anticipate her needs, offer assistance without being overbearing, and celebrate her achievements, no matter how small.

Our bond has deepened through shared experiences, creating a unique connection that transcends traditional roles. Liz's courage in the face of trials has inspired us all, and her resolution to live life to the fullest is a constant source of motivation. As she continues to evolve and grow, we will offer support, guidance, and unconditional love.

In the end, compassion, care, and belief in one another make a difference. By prioritizing the well-being of our loved ones and advocating for their needs, we create a foundation for resilience and hope. And so, as we endure and embrace the complexities of life together, we find strength in our faith in God and the power of the human spirit. My faith has never been stronger.

"Therefore, I tell you, whatever you ask for in prayer, believe that you have received it, and it will be yours."

-(Mark 11:24)

"This is the confidence we have in approaching God: that if we ask anything according to His will, He hears us."

-(John 5:14)

As we continue to seek His will in prayer, we can rest assured that He will provide the guidance and support we need to navigate life's challenges.

From the Care Pages

2-16-20

She is still unstable and we don't know brain function yet. She has been off the sedative since 1800 and has not woken up yet. They still don't know what is causing her heart to beat irregularly at times. She is maxed out on the pressors too to keep her BP up. My mom made it from Mexico tonight so that's good. We all just feel helpless at this point. Her kids who are 7 and 10 are doing ok but that's going to be short lived. I asked about transfer to Spectrum but she's too unstable and there's nothing they would do differently at this point. She does have cardiomyopathy and her EF is 10-20% which is not good. They will do EEG in the morning and that will determine next steps. Her potassium has been running very high too in the 6-7 range. We just need lots of prayers.

Just to update everyone: liz had a hysterectomy last tues and was recovering well. Last night she was

2.16

watching tv and told Liam to go get Pat and when he returned she was unresponsive. He called 911 and started cpr. They shocked her twice at home and in the ambulance. We all thought for sure it was a blood clot from surgery. Well they haven't found that at all and think this was an unrelated cardiac arrhythmia. Her heart is enlarged as well.

We are trying to limit visitors and phone calls and texts because there is a lot going on. So please know it may take us a bit to respond at times especially since there are lots of doctors in and out.

2-18-2020

Update: monday was a better day after a rough night of electrolyte imbalances. She has now been off sedation since 6am and has not woken up. She is off all other meds and is only receiving amiodarone to control heart rhythm. Her pupils are still reactive and she did some moving but it sounds like maybe it was posturing. She did move her head tonight when her husband came in the room talking about the kids. And i tickled her foot and she pulled it away. She also didn't like her airway being suctioned. They are giving her more time before doing an EEG since she has had some very small neuro improvement. Renal function is still good and liver enzymes are elevated but that's expected. This could be causing the narcotics and propafol longer to clear. My sister has never tolerated narcotics well so she's going to clear on her own schedule....and she never does anything by the book. We are keeping visitors to a minimum and low stimulation so her brain

2-14-20

can heal as much as possible. We really can't know anything more until we can establish what her neuro status is. I still feel like i need to wake up from this nightmare.

It has been the longest week of my family's life. Liz has made progress but they truly are baby steps. She does seem to track you with her eyes and focus on you when you talk to her. She blinks but does not follow any commands yet. She is now responding to pain. MRI confirmed 2 large and 4 small strokes on the left side of her brain. This is causing paralysis of the right side. Brain stem looks ok. My cousin who is a neurologist came to see her yesterday and felt encouraged, but like everyone else has said, she needs time. We were so thankful for her input. The unknown of how much she will recover is so hard to accept. She has been running a fever so some infection is present. She has a lot of movement in the left arm and was grabbing at her face last night so the nurse did put a loose restraint on that arm, just to avoid any excitement overnight 😐. My brother stayed both nights auth her this weekend to give me a break but I'll be back for the

next 3 before I need to return to work.
We are all accepting this is the new
normal for awhile and supporting Pat and
the kids as much we can. They are hoping
to extubate mid-week to see how well
she can breathe and oxygenate on her
own. We know she's been breathing over
the ventilator all along but don't know if
she could sustain breathing without some
assistance. The nursing care has been
amazing, we are so thankful for that. And
all the friends and family who've brought
food and offered to help with anything
has been overwhelming. Hug your loved
ones, you never know what the day may
bring.

2-26-2020

Today is a big day for Liz. They are planning to place a tracheostomy tube around noon and after this she will get a feeding tube placed in the next couple days. She is making little progress everyday is moving much more on the left side and starting to make some more movements on the right. We feel like when you look at her she focuses on you and wants to ask what's happening. We hope with the breathing to doubt she'll be able to use her mouth and possibly mouth some words to us. Pray for Pat and the kids, who still have not seen her, we are hoping they will be able to once the breathing tube is removed. The goal is to hopefully get her to a rehab unit maybe by the weekend.

Wed/Thurs update: today was a rough day emotionally. Neuro did not have positive things to say. I was not here but everyone felt like he said she was not going to recover past where she is now. MRI got canceled and not reordered, not sure why. Dr. Bennett who did her hysterectomy last week has been very involved as a friend and doctor, he spoke with Dr. Farooq who specializes in stroke mgmt at Mercy in Grand Rapids, and he's going to look at MRI that was reordered for Thursday. She has done a few more things since i left wed morning. Definitely trying to cough and has had some head and jaw movement. She is now getting some nutrition as well. She has a clot in her arm at an old IV site so is still on heparin. But receiving all other meds thru her NG tube. Sounds like chest tube could come out today. So all that is left is to get her brain on track. We are being told that she needs at least a week before we will really know. Thank you everyone for all the prayers and offers to help with kids and meals. We are lucky to have such great people surrounding us.

My Account

Menu

Journal Entry by Emily Quiney — February 28, 2020

It has been a long 2 weeks for Liz and family. Liz had an uncomplicated hysterectomy on Feb 11 and was home recovering well. She was watching TV with her son on Sat, Feb 15, when she asked him to get her husband. Pat found her unresponsive and called 911. He immediately started CPR and within minutes EMS was there and able to take over. She was taken to Mercy Health in Muskegon via ambulance and proceeded to have another 6 episodes of ventricular fibrillation. Once she was stabilized it was discovered she had also suffered numerous strokes on the left side associated with the multiple cardiac arrests. She was transferred to the ICU and placed on the ventilator, cardiac monitoring, and multiple medications. During this we were hard at work trying to get my mom home, as she was in Mexico on vacation. After 24hrs she was at the bedside, along with all of her siblings, father, and husband.

She was very unstable for the first 48hrs and remained sedated at this time. Once they turned off the sedation, we were hopeful she would wake up. Well, in true Liz fashion, she took her time. She slowly began to open her eyes but didn't seem to be focusing. By Feb 22, she had some positive neurological signs, including corneal reflex and pupil reactivity. We were then waiting on a pain response which came a few days later.

So far the cause of her arrest has not been determined. Due to some cardiac arrhythmias she has had, the plan to is place a pacemaker/defibrillator.

Liz has made slow progress, but all we can do is wait. She is young and her prognosis is good, but it will take time. How much? We don't know. Wednesday they removed the endotracheal tube and put in a tracheotomy, then transferred her from the ICU to Long Term Acute Care (LTAC). She also received a feeding tube yesterday. She is moving her left arm and leg, her head, and has also made some small movements with the right arm and hand. She opens and closes her eyes on demand, and seems to recognize voices and will focus on you. With the things out of her mouth and nose, she SMILED!!!! This was the best thing yet!

We will post updates as we are able, but please know the progress is naturally going to be slow. My hope with this page is that people can keep updated without bothering the family. While we know everyone is concerned and we do feel the love, texts an phone calls all day long is exhausting for everyone.

TOP

  https://www.caringbridge.org/visit/lizstocker/journal

80
My Account

Menu

Journal Entry by Patrick Stocker — February 28, 2020

TGIF - Liz is resting and recovering today in her new room. Doc's have taken her off the ventilator this afternoon for a trial run. Kids looking forward to their 1st visit this weekend.

32 Hearts

9 Comments

❤ Heart   💬 Comment   ➢ Share

Write a comment...

View all comments

February 28, 2020

Journal Entry by Emily Quiney — February 28, 2020

Liz has 2 kids, Paige is 10 and Liam is 7. They were home at the time of her cardiac arrest. They have not seen her yet. We were strongly cautioned against them seeing her in the ICU hooked up to so many tubes and monitors as this can be very scary for kids. Now that her face looks like "mom" we are hoping they can see her this weekend. Please pray for them and Pat as they take this next step.

23 Hearts

5 Comments

❤ Heart   💬 Comment   ➢ Share

Write a comment...

View all comments

TOP

  10/20/2020, 1:54 Pl

80

My Account

Menu

Journal Entry by kathy bailey — March 4, 2020

Liz amazes me. As my first journal entry I am in awe with the love, support and prayers we have received from everywhere. She had a good day today, up in the cardiac chair twice which totally exhausts her. She smiles through it all, confused but very lucid at times. Trying to figure out what is going on but now, I think realized that she is in the hospital and she is trying to figure out what has happened. She wanted to know where the kids were today and she was satisfied they were in school. Mark asked her if she would like him to bring his guitar and serenade her and she replied no with a smile. Liz has a great sense of humor and that still shows. Her smiles keep me going and I just want to keep her going. She is strong. We are sharing this journey.

33 Hearts   14 Comments

❤ Heart   💬 Comment   ↗ Share

Write a comment...

View all comments

Donate to CaringBridge

TOP

80

My Account   Menu

Journal Entry by Patrick Stocker — February 28, 2020

TGIF - Liz is resting and recovering today in her new room. Doc's have taken her off the ventilator this afternoon for a trial run. Kids looking forward to their 1st visit this weekend.

32 Hearts   9 Comments

♡ Heart   ▢ Comment   ↗ Share

Write a comment...

View all comments

February 28, 2020

Journal Entry by Emily Quiney — February 28, 2020

Liz has 2 kids, Paige is 10 and Liam is 7. They were home at the time of her cardiac arrest. They have not seen her yet. We were strongly cautioned against them seeing her in the ICU hooked up to so many tubes and monitors as this can be very scary for kids. Now that her face looks like "mom" we are hoping they can see her this weekend. Please pray for them and Pat as they take this next step.

23 Hearts   5 Comments

♡ Heart   ▢ Comment   ↗ Share

Write a comment...

View all comments

TOP

80

My Account

Menu

Journal Entry by Mary Blaicher — February 29, 2020

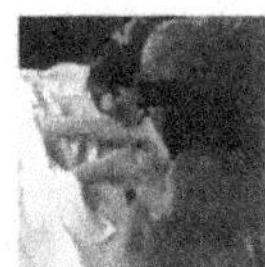

I visited Liz this morning, and WOW! What a difference between seeing her in the evenings and during the day when she's more alert. It was very encouraging to see that she did know who I was, was all smiles, mouths answers to some questions, mouths "I love you" and even "laughs" at my bad jokes. Her personality is definitely there, and she kissed me goodbye.

She is off all medication drips and will be getting any by injection/feeding tube now. She is also off the vent and just has some oxygen going into the tracheostomy tube.

Her smile is hers and is even on both sides, which is encouraging that her swallowing is normal, as well, but we will not know for sure until the trach is out (no idea on when that would be...didn't ask).

Pat brought the kids to see her today, and it went very well. She was clearly very happy to see them and hear about what's going on at school and in their lives. Paige & Bailey even painted her toenails! Liz was not keen on me taking a picture of her smiling (I'll keep working on that ;)). so here's one of the toenails being painted instead!

If you'd like to send a card to Liz, please mail to her at my mom's house, and we'll be happy to take to the hospital, read them to her, and tape up on the wall. Feel free to contact one of us for the address.

Keep the prayers coming--they are working!! Praise God!

28 Hearts

11 Comments

❤ Heart   💬 Comment   ↪ Share

TOP

https://www.caringbridge.org/visit/lizstocker/journal

80
My Account

Menu

Journal Entry by Patrick Stocker — March 3, 2020

Happy Tuesday, Liz continues to progress in a positive direction. Kids have been up to visit 3 days in row! She is smiling and holding the kids hands as they discus their day.. ☺.. Hope is in the air!

You and 31 others

11 Comments

❤ Heart   💬 Comment   ↗ Share

Write a comment...

View all comments

TOP

10/20/2020, 1:54 P

https://www.caringbridge.org/visit/lizstocker/journal

80

My Account

Menu

Journal Entry by kathy bailey — March 4, 2020

Liz amazes me. As my first journal entry I am in awe with the love, support and prayers we have received from everywhere. She had a good day today, up in the cardiac chair twice which totally exhausts her. She smiles through it all, confused but very lucid at times. Trying to figure out what is going on but now, I think realized that she is in the hospital and she is trying to figure out what has happened. She wanted to know where the kids were today and she was satisfied they were in school. Mark asked her if she would like him to bring his guitar and serenade her and she replied no with a smile. Liz has a great sense of humor and that still shows. Her smiles keep me going and I just want to keep her going. She is strong. We are sharing this journey.

33 Hearts   14 Comments

Heart   Comment   Share

Write a comment...

View all comments

Donate to CaringBridge

TOP

10/20/2020, 1:54 Pl

80

My Account

Menu

Journal Entry by kathy bailey — March 7, 2020

Is it Saturday already? Liz is sleeping peacefully at the moment after being up in chair for a while and her morning activities are behind her. Kids and Pat just left for a while. My wonderful step daughter -in -law Elizabeth is taking care of Marys kids for me and then I will go home and take them to see new baby sister..Emma, who was born yesterday. Liz loved seeing pictures of her this morning. Such an arrange of emotions flood my day between a new baby and Liz gaining strength everyday and they are both beautiful. Thank you everyone for the beautiful cards and prayers..We are forever thankful!

32 Hearts

11 Comments

 Heart   Comment   Share

Write a comment...

View all comments

TOP

https://www.caringbridge.org/visit/lizstocker/journal

185

80
My Account

Menu

Journal Entry by Patrick Stocker — March 6, 2020

TGIF - another week removed. Today was a really great day in the life of the Stocker's.
Liz was all smiles today, she really looked great and showed her pearly whites to
everyone. The kids visited, told her about school, friends, books and even about Sully.
Liz held their hands and really listened to every word. We had family and friends stop
over and visit, showing how much we all love Liz. Also, we became an Aunt and Uncle
again today, way to go Mary & Paul. God really blessed us today...enjoy your
weekend....Patrick

31 Hearts

2 Comments

Heart   Comment   Share

Write a comment...

View all comments

TOP

10/20/2020, 1:54 PI

80
My Account

≡
Menu

Journal Entry by kathy bailey — March 9, 2020

Hard to verbalize this day. Liz was sleepy this morning when I arrived and not ready to tackle the day. But soon she is up in the cardiac chair which allows her to sit up comfortably. She becomes much more communicative and wants to know where she is and what has happened to her. I go through this with her daily and I don't sugar coat it but leave out some of it. She says she is sorry Mark and I had to come home early from Mexico. Really Liz????is there any other place I could possibly be right now. I had to leave for an hour and came back and she was sitting on the side of the bed, with assistance of course, but a big smile when she saw me. She brushed her own teeth today and after trying to endure daytime TV, it was time for some Little River Band on my Spotify and damn if she did not mouth the words verbatim. And then Lionel Richie 's All Night Long...and yes we are going to have a party Liz when you get out of here.

Best part of all was they downsized the trachea and they were able to put the Passy Muir Valve on while Pat and kids were there. I will witness that tomorrow. Another best part of our lives is that Emma Katherine is such a beautiful and healthy baby and she brings joy to Liz's eyes. So many gifts today.

35 Hearts   18 Comments

❤ Heart   💬 Comment   ↪ Share

Write a comment...

View all comments

TOP

80

My Account

Menu

Journal Entry by kathy bailey — March 13, 2020

Liz had a good day yesterday. The trach has been removed which is another step in the road to recovery. Unfortunately, there are restrictions being imposed at the hospital. I realize these are necessary but Liz will be unable to see Paige and Liam until this ban is lifted. It's an important part of her recovery but it would be awful for Liz to be exposed to anything even a cold at this point. So thank God for FaceTime. Liz is only able to have one visitor at a time so we will have to plan any visits at this point. That being said Liz is speaking and is doing therapy as tolerated. She is considered a low stimulation patient as it will help her focus at the tasks she has now and ahead of her. We are so thankful for your continued prayers and this great country where we have choices in our health care. The care she has received has been wonderful. God has placed the talents of many physicians, nurses and therapists in her life. May God's blessings continue to watch over Liz and all of us who love her.

29 Hearts

3 Comments

Heart   Comment   Share

Write a comment...

View all comments

TOP

80
My Account

Menu

Journal Entry by Emily Quiney — March 19, 2020

Today was a big day for Liz!!! She was transferred to Mary Free Bed in Grand Rapids and she now gets 1 visitor....so Pat was there when she arrived, and as anyone can imagine, she was quite emotional when she saw him. She hasn't seen anyone but medical staff for a week, and while she is now allowed 1 visitor, it has to be the same person, so mom and children will still not be allowed to visit. A few things we know she has been trying to do, yesterday she attempted to sign her name with her right hand, and it had a good resemblance to her writing. She has also been spending more time in the chair and her speech is really improving. She also was able to tell someone her cell number!

I am working on getting an address so people can mail cards and notes to her, and I ask that everyone adhere to the visitor policy since you will be turned away if you try. This will be a very exhausting place for her as there will be rigorous therapy and she will need as much rest as possible so she can get home to her family.

Thanks again for all the prayers----they are working!!!

42 Hearts

17 Comments

Heart   Comment   Share

Write a comment...

View all comments

TOP

10/20/2020, 1:54 PI

80

My Account

Menu

Journal Entry by Patrick Stocker — March 23, 2020

As the world around us changes by the moment due to the Coronavirus, Liz's world also continues to change...for the better! At Mary-Free Bed she has 3 hours of therapy each day - physical/speech/occupational, very exhausting but very exciting all in the same as her recovery continues to see results. Also, as you can see in the picture from today, she passed her swallow test today with flying colors and has no restrictions, never have I seen somebody enjoy hospital food so much..😊..Thanks again for all the prayers and support, they continue to work.

33 Hearts

20 Comments

🖤 Heart   💬 Comment   ➥ Share

Write a comment...

View all comments

80

My Account

Menu

Journal Entry by kathy bailey — March 23, 2020

Even though I am unable to see Liz right now, I wake up everyday and know we are one day closer to bringing Liz home. I truly believe that her recovery has been miraculous thus far and thank all of you for your daily prayers and constant support. I have two parts of Liz with me everyday, Paige and Liam. I am so thankful that Patrick is with her everyday encouraging her every step of the way. He is her gift in these difficult steps of recovery.

29 Hearts   5 Comments

🦅 Heart   💬 Comment   ↪ Share

Write a comment...

View all comments

TOP

80

My Account   Menu

Journal Entry by Patrick Stocker — March 27, 2020

First week at MFB and WOW, what a great place to be. The staff has Liz completing at least 3 hours of rehab a day. This week alone she has passed her swallow test and has no diet restrictions (Eating Anything and Everything). Physical therapy has her walking and climbing steps....yes steps! Today she hits the treadmill. Occupational has her dressing herself every morning and working with her fine motor skills each afternoon. Liz got a chance to work with a therapy dog this afternoon, she really enjoyed this change, maybe Sully can become her therapy dog? Looking forward to the weekend, I'm praying that everyone is safe and spends time with their loved ones...Patrick

30 Hearts   8 Comments

🖤 Heart   💬 Comment   ↪ Share

Write a comment...

View all comments

TOP

https://www.caringbridge.org/visit/lizstocker/journa

80

My Account

Menu

Journal Entry by Patrick Stocker — April 2, 2020

April has finally arrived, I'm sure everyone felt March would never end....Liz is still on target to come home on the 15th. She has been working so hard and making huge gains everyday, even her sarcasm is back to fell strength.. 😄 😄 ..the kids are are very excited to see har soon as the hospital is still on visitation restrictions. Thanks again for all the thoughts and prayers everyone has given, please enjoy your own family and be safe during this global crisis...Patrick

21 Hearts

4 Comments

♥ Heart   💬 Comment   ↗ Share

Write a comment...

View all comments

TOP

10/20/2020, 1:54 PM

80

My Account

Menu

Journal Entry by Mary Blaicher — April 28, 2020

Hi everyone!

Liz has been home for a couple of weeks now and things are good. She is getting lots of exercise around the neighborhood and with therapy!

I wanted to share an update about her brain recovery, as many of you have been asking or have spoken with her recently and have questions.

Liz's biggest struggle as far as her brain recovery goes is her memory. Her short-term memory is almost non-existent at this time, and her long-term memory has holes. She feels like she has been "gone" for 3 years, and there are things--large things and small details--that are confusing to her on a daily basis. She wakes up every day almost as if it's the first day she's woken up. This can be very frustrating for her, so please do continue to keep her recovery in your prayers. It can take up to 18 months for the brain to heal as much as it's going to, so this is a very long road, and we are hopeful these parts can be healed and memories restored.

All that to say that if you speak with her, she will likely tell you that she just woke up today and may not remember your conversation. She is constantly trying to decipher real life from false things her brain is telling her. So, do not be alarmed if certain things don't make sense at this time, or if she calls you without remembering that you spoke recently.

All in all, she is happy to be home with her family, and we look forward to her continued progress.

We appreciate all of your continued prayers and your love for Liz and her family.

20 Hearts   8 Comments

♡ Heart   ⬜ Comment   ↪ Share

Write a comment...   TOP

 80

My Account

Menu

Journal Entry by kathy bailey — May 28, 2020

A birthday was celebrated on Memorial Day, Silently I have thought this birthday may have never happened and wondered how we all would get through that day BUT Yeah!!! Liz turned 39 on May 25th. The Spring Lakers gathered with Mark and I and celebrated in style with Liz. Although still feeling a bit exhausted from her defibrillator placement she managed to smile and enjoy the afternoon. A socially distanced visit by Aunt Patty and Uncle Paul for a few minutes was a surprise for Liz. So wonderful to finally see them after a couple months.

We had some great strides at therapy. Told her not to use the walker anymore for her walks. Get rid of it! Only has to wear her support for her right leg when she goes on a walk or uneven ground. She has set some great goals for herself and is working hard on the tools she has to regain her short term memory. She came over after therapy for lunch at my house and for me it was like nothing had ever happened. We just chatted and she asked me questions about going forward and I reassured her that with time things will only improve. "You've got this Liz!"

She does not think of herself but longs to fulfill her role as wife, mom, sister and daughter. I assure you she will get there and has accomplished so much in such a short time. The greatest joy for me is that she is walking in the front door, on her own, and saying "Hi Mom!"

Thank you many times over Patrick for being a wonderful husband and father.. And lastly thanks to all of you for your continued prayers and support. God has listened.

15 Hearts

5 Comments

Heart   Comment   Share

Write a comment...

View all comments

TOP

10/20/2020, 1:54 PI